**Political Science in
Population Studies**

Political Science in Population Studies

Richard L. Clinton
University of North Carolina

William S. Flash
University of North Carolina

R. Kenneth Godwin
Oregon State University

Lexington Books
D.C. Heath and Company
Lexington, Massachusetts
Toronto   London

First drafts of these papers served as discussion material at a Political Science/Population Workshop partially supported by funds provided by the United States Agency for International Development (Contract No. csd/2507 to the University of North Carolina Population Center). The viewpoints expressed herein are those of the authors and editors and do not necessarily represent those of USAID. Reproduction in whole or in part permitted for any purpose of the U.S. Government.

Published simultaneously in Canada.

Printed in the United States of America.

International Standard Book Number: 0-669-82057-1

Library of Congress Catalog Card Number: 75-186337

Table of Contents

List of Figures

List of Tables

Foreword

Better understanding of the causes and implications of human population phenomena, and more effective application of such knowledge, will require the mobilization of concepts and methods from many of today's academic disciplines. The involvement of such disciplines in this complex field is emerging slowly. One problem is that in any field an existing intellectual priesthood, such as that noted by Bergman in the present book, may resist new entrants. In the case of political science, perhaps a preoccupation with defining its own modern identity has also slowed the rediscovery of some of its ancestral haunts.

Political philosophers of yore were deeply concerned with the population dimensions of politics, as cited by Lipsitz. On the other hand, the beginnings of modern population studies undertaken by Petty and Graunt in the 1600s were termed "political arithmetic." The modern English usage of the word "population" was even introduced by a consummate politician-scientist, Francis Bacon. More recently, Spengler, Lorimer, Eldridge, Glass, and others have discussed general aspects of population policies, but world attention to population phenomena has been more preoccupied with implications for such matters as women's emancipation, economic development, and health. Now population patterns are being viewed increasingly as more than "exogenous" variables and as manipulable, interactive factors which can profoundly influence the quality of life. Concern with the many political implications can be expected to rise rapidly. This is the emerging opportunity and challenge to political scientists.

The Department of Political Science at the University of North Carolina at Chapel Hill is a pioneer in exploring this new frontier of knowledge with a systematic program of studies and research and training. Population factors are found to touch on and to illuminate many of the existing, specialized areas of political studies. How best to refer to this new dimension within the discipline? Weiner's suggestion of "political demography" seems too confining; more elegant perhaps would be an application of the term "demogenics," as used by Saunders in this volume. How best to organize further knowledge about interactions between population and political variables, to facilitate research and, very importantly, to help link such knowledge with that emerging from other disciplines? What kinds of newer concepts and methods may have to be developed by political scientists to deal with population factors? What can such research hope to offer to policymakers, and when? This first book-length treatment of the population field by political scientists raises these and many other questions. It should be a landmark for the enrichment of political science and for enlargement of our understanding of human affairs.

Moye W. Freymann

Introduction

William S. Flash

An introduction to the politics of population is most appropriately expressed as a challenge to the profession of political science. The nature of the challenge is no less than this: to recognize and in concert with society to act upon the demographic realities of worldwide social upheaval. But what essential role is assignable to political science per se? If political science exists to inform social governance, then most especially the profession must rise to the challenge posed by radically potent forces of population growth and change now manifest on a worldwide scale. Neither the worn verities of classical political theory, the latter-day methodologies of the behavioralists, nor least of all the attack on contemporary elite society by the profession's activists—no school of thought within political science can escape this challenge to the discipline's established wisdom as well as to its capability for creativity.

Fortunately responses within the profession are beginning to emerge. Among such, a small group of American political scientists with widely divergent disciplinary interests came together in December 1971, to submit draft papers to mutual scrutiny and criticism in a roundtable workshop at the University of North Carolina.[1] Out of these discussions, the eight chapters of this volume have subsequently developed.[2] Workshop drafts have been either markedly revised or completely rewritten, with one exception: the opening challenge to the profession by Lyle Saunders from the viewpoint of policy action needs abroad. Saunders' statement represents the cutting edge of challenge opening up well beyond workshop walls rich possibilities of response as well as the pressing necessity to explore more deeply the full nature of the challenge itself.

Surely we must begin by admitting that in this world of academic specialization there is indeed little really new under the sun: the study of politics and aggregates of people really has a substantial and diverse lineage. Wherein, then, is the urgency of today's demographic challenge to modern political science? As Dr. Freymann suggests in his preface above, the urgency for political science is in the urgency of numbers and the now radical dimensions of population growth, size, and distribution with their overwhelming implications for social survival and well-being. At its simplest (and most complex) the urgency, like the demographic condition itself, is a matter of exponential power. Recognition of that power and the complexities of its governance lies at the heart of political science (and with those who would profess it.)

Professor Peter Bachrach's characteristic recognition of power[3] has led him (chapter 2) to identify elements in the American "mobilization of bias" just as critically comparable in their implications for population policy as for poverty and other significant social policies which lack effective constituencies for political action. In conceptual approach as well as strategy recommendations, he suggests an unexplored avenue of population policy analysis that should yield results useful to political science as well as to societies themselves under the impact of population dynamics.[4]

Just as Bachrach would deny to the effective political scientist an antiseptic sanctuary from the realities of power, Professor Theodore Lowi also deals (chapter 3) with the unavoidability of coercion as the key ingredient of alternative options in the political processes through which population planning and control may be undertaken by government. He points out that the power impact of "intentional population growth control" policies, for example, not only would cut across the wide spectrum of vested interests in related social policy fields, but would in the long run shape basic political processes themselves and their meaning in the evolution of American self-government. Lowi's conceptual approach also denies sanctuary to the political scientist and instead urges him to grasp the nettles of power realities if full and honest assessment of population policy outcomes is what is owed to society.

But is power per se at the heart of social conflict? Or does the heart of contemporary social conflict draw its potency from the psychic wellsprings of society's evolving, modernizing, and constantly accelerating growth and mobility, with society everywhere intensifying as well as fleeing from its own density, cherishing as well as challenging its own values? Professor Alden Lind probes these sources of conflict (chapter 4), relating them to population factors in systematically interdependent and multidimensional terms. What are the political implications, he asks, when physical space, under demographic impact, becomes psychic space?

Thus, in political terms the ghost of *Lebensraum* returns. Conflicts internal to society turn outward into terms of external aggrandizement. The calculus of power among nations is assessed and reassessed. Concepts and empirical realities of power and population combine to emerge as measures of "effective population" by Professor A.F.K. Organski and his colleagues (chapter 5). In their hands, indices of economic productivity and political mobilization rework the traditional profiles of international power comparisons among populous and not so populous nations of the world. The relativity of power constitutes the significant interface, the full meaning of which extends well beyond demographic variables.

Challenges to relative capabilities among nations are also the concern of Professor Jason Finkle's comparison of family planning program performance in India and Pakistan (chapter 6). He suggests that within one nation as compared with another the complex interdependencies of political structure, ideology, processes, and modes of survival can be seen as a multidimensional matrix determining capability of program performance. Urgencies of Pakistan's national economic planning (to which family planning was originally tied) sweep everything before it, including sooner rather than later the stability of political rule itself. In comparing Pakistan's family planning program with India's, have we political scientists nothing more useful to offer than Aesop's wisdom of the tortoise and the hare? Must we not accept Finkle's lead and work to develop further empirical studies comparing political and administrative capabilities in the diversity of settings within which population policies need to reach effectuation?

But effectuation for what? Population policies are not ends in themselves. They express instrumental values rather than primary or ultimate values. As Professor Lipsitz's essay suggests (chapter 7), in reflecting upon certain of the traditional questions and answers in Western political philosophy, perhaps the really basic challenge of the population behemoth is to identify anew the value questions central to the governance of mankind as this process is now recognized in its full ecological setting.[5] What extant political philosophy offers us a theory for a too-many-peopled world or for politically demographic consequences of superabundance and underdevelopment? Posed as challenges to political scientists, are the questions Saunders raises in chapter 1 *really* "demogenic" questions? Surely in root causes they are ecologic and not "simply" demographic. But where in the workshops of political theory are these and more basic conceptual adaptations and redefinitions being shaped?

Finally, at the working level of practical evaluation, surely the political science profession has the responsiveness and substantive ability to pitch in with the other social sciences and develop working wisdom beyond that of Aesop. Or, as in the Pakistan government's initially exclusive embrace of the IUD, have political scientists no practical wisdom with which to anticipate and counter the seductive force of a technological "solution"? A technological panacea to a social and political problem seems a contradiction in terms. Can we really say no more than that? Have the technologists in the field of public administration and political process nothing more to say to desperate societies perilously tempted by technological "solutions"?

All the papers in this volume implicitly speak to what is in fact an evaluation crisis dwelling deep within contemporary society and, by reflection, within the political science profession. When confronted with radical forces of the magnitude of population growth and movement, how can societies evaluate themselves and the policies with which intervention is to be attempted? For better or worse all such intervention strategies in this cybernetic world are now both intensely personal and potently political. Are the facts, explanations, predictions, and ultimately the necessary value judgments[6] to be developed *without* benefit of an open and regenerative political science? That is the challenge offered to the profession by the authors and to which their papers make an initial response. Their work constitutes a most fitting introduction to the urgent politics of population.

Notes

1. Sponsored jointly by the University's Department of Political Science and the Carolina Population Center, the workshop was partly supported through a grant from the U.S. Agency for International Development.

2. Monograph publication of a ninth paper is anticipated, "Political Implications of Cityward Migration in Japan," by James W. White.

3. See Peter Bachrach and Morton S. Baratz, *Power and Poverty: Theory and Practice* (New York: Oxford University Press, 1970).

4. Following Bachrach's lead, Elihu Bergman and William S. Flash have presented "The American Population Policy Process: Some Critical Insights" to the 1971 annual meetings of the American Political Science Association, Chicago, Illinois, September 10, 1971.

5. See Peter A. Corning "The Biological Bases of Behavior and Some Implications for Political Science," *World Politics* 23, no. 3 (April 1971): 321-70.

6. See Norton E. Long's introduction and especially the first two chapters of Eugene J. Meehan's *Value Judgement and Social Science: Structure and Processes* (Homewood, Illinois: Dorsey Press, 1969).

**Political Science in
Population Studies**

1

Action Needs: The Relevance of Political Research

Lyle Saunders

Demogenic Phenomena and Population Planning

Since the 1950s and increasingly during the 60s, people and governments have begun to perceive and to be concerned with various phenomena that may be classified as demogenic—i.e., as originating in population processes. An incomplete listing of these would include such phenomena as:

—Rapid population growth, as in India and mainland China, which annually grow by about 13 million each and together contribute nearly two-fifths of the world's total annual growth
—Population size, as exemplified by the two giants, India and China, which include half a billion and three-quarters of a billion people respectively and jointly contain a third of all the world's population, and by the lesser giants among developing nations, Pakistan and Indonesia, each of which is well over 100 million
—Dependency ratios, especially the preponderance of dependents under fifteen years of age, which typically runs between 43 and 48 percent in the developing countries
—Uneven distribution, as seen in such factors as rapid urbanization, high population density adjacent to areas of low density as in Indonesia, and the coastal concentrations in the United States, as revealed in the 1970 census counts
—The precarious balance between food production and population growth, relieved somewhat, but perhaps only temporarily, by the "green" revolution
—The dampening effects of population parameters—e.g., size, growth, distribution, dependency—on development progress
—The growing awareness of the environmental implications of the combination of population growth, population concentration, and rapid industrialization

In response to rising concern about these and other problem areas, governments in both the developed and developing regions have begun to take action. It is beginning to be possible to identify in some countries sets of related decisions and actions that collectively could be defined as population planning. Included would be such areas as:

1

–The formulation, adoption, and implementation of various kinds of population policy
–The inclusion of population considerations in all phases of development planning, emphasizing especially the two-way influence between development factors and population factors
–Family planning, i.e., support to voluntary birth control by reproducing couples through the provision of information, materials, and services for contraception, sterilization, and abortion
–Attempts to influence or control population movements and distribution both internally and across national boundaries
–Changes in legal provisions governing marriage and divorce; (the People's Republic of China has apparently had some success with its effort to delay the age of marriage for population reasons; Italy has just liberalized its divorce laws, but probably not for any anticipated effect on fertility)
–Manipulation of tax and welfare policies to reduce their pronatalist and increase any possible antinatalist influences
–Changes in the status of women

According to a recent count by the Population Council, twenty-four developing nations (including the nonsovereign territory of Puerto Rico) that together encompass nearly 70 percent of the population of the developing areas now have population policies or programs. These include the four developing nations with over 100 million each and seven of the ten that have populations between 25 and 100 million. An additional fifteen nations, with populations up to 25 million each, provide support to family planning programs but have no explicit policies. Only one country, India, has a policy or government-supported program antedating 1960; all the rest began their population activity in the 1960s except the four countries that have adopted policies only this year.

In all countries with policies and programs the major vehicle for dealing directly with rapid population growth and indirectly at related problems has been family planning. It is too soon to know if family planning can work and, if so, what are the necessary and sufficient conditions for it to succeed. Reasonably hard evidence from Hong Kong and Taiwan indicates that family planning programs have contributed to fertility decline in those countries. Such evidence is not available for other nations, and, in the absence of systematic evaluation of program efforts in most of them, such progress as seems to be made has to be taken on faith.

There are two schools of thought with respect to family planning. One group doubts that it can ever be successful because individuals will follow their own desires and preferences rather than considering societal needs when deciding the number and timing of their children. Others argue that couples in developed countries already control their reproduction at a level near that required for negligible growth by voluntary decisions and actions, and that we can't know whether similar results could be achieved in developing countries because there has not been enough time to find out and because—for a variety of reasons, mainly political—no country has made anything near a maximum effort.

No one can be certain whether family planning will be able to bring down fertility rates rapidly and substantially in developing countries or what would be required if it could. My guess is that a minimum requirement would be all of the following, carried on over a fairly long period of time—say ten years at the least:

—Strong, continuing, in-depth political support. An essential ingredient is what Berelson has called "political will" coming from a group of high-level, respected, and powerful political leaders. No country, with the possible exception of Japan, has yet achieved it to the required degree

—Removal of legal restrictions on the import, transport, sale, and use of contraceptives. Some countries with national population policies and programs still prohibit or make difficult the importation and distribution of contraceptive supplies

—Legal sterilization (both male and female) and abortion on request. Dr. Christopher Tietze of the Population Council has pointed out that the safest and most effective form of birth control is a reasonably good contraceptive backed by abortion to take care of failures. Singapore legalized abortion early this year, and a bill to liberalize abortion is now under consideration in the Indian parliament. So far as I know, abortion is not legal in other developing countries. India and Pakistan have emphasized sterilizations, with India claiming to have done over six million up to August 1969. The only other countries that have reported over 100,000 are South Korea and Thailand

—Convenient, widespread and low-cost availability of birth control information, materials, and services through both public and private channels, including commercial distribution systems

—Minimization of pronatalist influences of government policies and maximization of antinatalist effects from policies

Most of the above essentials for successful family planning programs require political decisions and political acts. They also require a fair amount of political foresight and courage since many of these areas are believed to be sensitive and family planning is not likely to have a highly visible short-run payoff. Perhaps these considerations partly explain why no government has yet made a full commitment to family planning.

With the appearance of a large new area of government interest and activity concerned with a phenomenon widely believed to have ominous implications for human welfare—an area in which results are problematic and political risks likely to be high—one would think that social scientists concerned with governmental and political affairs would be attracted by the research problems and opportunities in the new area. But this does not seem to have happened. The rising awareness of rapid population increase and of its possibly wide-ranging consequences that has become evident since the 1950s and the assumption by governments of responsibility for trying to cope with that increase have added new dimensions to old problems and have created what must be formidable new problems for those who hold political office and wield political power. These problems require political decisions and actions that can have substantial political, as well as social and economic, consequences. To make the decisions and to take the actions wisely and rationally would seem to require new knowledge, including that which could be provided by political science research. But it is my impression—a superficial and uninformed one to be sure—that political scientists as a group have not yet begun to concern themselves with problems in the population area and are not now doing much research in this area.

As suggestive, but not necessarily conclusive evidence supporting this impression, I note the findings of my colleague, Edwin Driver, who recently surveyed social science departments in this country (and prior to that in India) to learn what they are doing or plan to do in teaching and research related to population policy. Driver found that none of the political science departments responding to his questions offered a course specifically on population, although several included population content as a minor component to other courses. He found, too, that only three of the twenty departments polled were interested to offer suggestions for research on population policy. His conclusion was that "the specialty of population studies has been of less importance in the teaching and research activities of political scientists than in those of any other social science discipline except psychology."[1] This seems somewhat strange to me, given what has been happening in other countries as well as the events in this country during the past few years. The rapidity with which public attitudes and legal enactments relating to abortion, for example have changed in this country would, I should think, constitute a phenomenon of considerable interest to students of political processes. Perhaps it does, and perhaps it is being adequately studied. One would hope that it is.

During much of the 1960s, I have been able to move about the world and to have the opportunity to observe the establishment, organization, and operation of population programs—mostly family planning—in a number of developing countries and to participate in some of the processes by which policies have been formulated and adopted and family planning programs established. During this experience I have gradually become aware of problem areas to which I believe systematic political science research could make useful contributions. I should like to list and comment briefly on some of these areas in the hope that some of them may have sufficient political science interest to stimulate workshop discussion. I can't say any of these *is* an area that political science should be studying. I can only raise the question, "Are they?" I do know that some of these are areas of considerable importance to population planning and that help from the social sciences is needed.

Policy Problem Areas

Population Policy—Definition, Formulation, Adoption, Implementation. I'm not
entirely clear about what constitutes population policy. I would define a policy
as an official statement that serves as a guide to some goal-oriented action. But it
would seem that policy may also be, in the absence of an explicit statement, an
inference from a set of actions that seem to lead in a given direction. I don't
know anything that is labelled U.S. population policy, although several presi-
dents in a row have made statements about population and indicated national
concern and possible action, Congress has passed legislation relevant to family
planning and other population matters, several government agencies are carrying
on family planning activity, and a secretary of HEW has made at least one
statement entitled "Department Policy on Population Dynamics, Fertility, Ste-
rility, and Family Planning." By contrast, Ghana has a document labelled *Ghana
Population Policy* that sets forth a proposed line of activity and the reasons
therefore. Colombia is defined by the Population Council as having no policy,
but its president signed the World Leaders' Statement on Population, and family
planning services are offered in government clinics by government workers. The
trend seems to be in the direction of explicit official statements, as exemplified
by the comprehensive statement of Ghana which goes beyond a decision to
provide information and the means to family planning in order to reduce fertility and expresses positive intentions toward: limiting morbidity and mortality,
promoting wider roles for women including expanded educational opportunities,
curtailing maternity benefits and children's allowances, guiding and reducing the
flow of internal migration, and restricting immigration. During 1970, explicit
policy statements were adopted by Indonesia, the Philippines, Thailand, and
Nigeria.

Until the 1950s national policies relevant to population tended to be pronatalist and to reflect the viewpoint that large and growing populations contribute to and may be necessary for national prestige, power, or prosperity. Some
countries, notably Brazil and a number of African nations, still subscribe to this
view, at least to the extent that statements by national leaders reveal national
policy. But in the past decade statements and actions have begun to reflect
antinatalist positions as nations have become concerned with the possibly limiting effects of rapid population growth on development goals and aspirations.

The formulation, expression, adoption, and implementation of population
policies should be of interest to political scientists.[a] Within a single decade some
forty nations have adopted policies and programs or have begun to provide
government support to private population planning efforts. (Frequently, as in

[a]Perhaps they are or are coming to be. One indication may be the interest of the American
Association for the Advancement of Science which announced sessions at the annual
meeting this month on policy sciences, a new supradiscipline devoted to the study and
improvement of policy making.

the case of Nigeria, these latter efforts are rationalized as contributions towards better health and welfare for mothers and children, with no population effect intended.) Other countries with large and rapidly growing populations—e.g., Brazil, Burma, Mexico, Ethiopia, and South Africa—have not acted. Why the difference? Are there discoverable sets of political factors that account for the decisions to adopt and implement antinatalist policies? If so, are such factors general or country specific? What are the relevant political differences between countries that adopt positive policies and programs to reduce fertility and those that are merely permissive? Is there an invariant sequence of stages of the policy formation and adoption process? Can political conditions be identified that are either necessary or sufficient for a positive decision on fertility-reducing activity? How are decisions made and policies formulated? How can political will be strengthened once a policy is adopted? What political considerations determine the nature of implementing activities? Can policy decisions be predicted? If so, what data are needed for such predictions? Is there anything special about decision making in the population field as compared to other fields? If so, what is it and what are its implications?

These may not be answerable or even researchable questions. But the issues they relate to are important both for our time and for the future, and they should not be neglected.

Political Advantages and Disadvantages of Government Action in Population Planning. What do political leaders have to gain or lose by adopting population policies or supporting or not supporting population programs? The payoffs from family planning (assuming there are any) only begin after some years, and even then they are likely to be disguised (something prevented, something not spent) and only statistically visible. Nonborn children do not cast very dark shadows, and even with the most highly successful of family planning programs there are going to be a lot more people around in most countries in coming years than there are now. And, with a growing population base, reductions in the rate of growth may not make much difference in the absolute numbers of increase as compared to that of recent years. Added to these politically discouraging considerations are the further ones that family planning is concerned with the sensitive area of sexual behavior, that reproduction is widely regarded as a private matter, that high fertility has been the normal state of most populations throughout history and is almost everywhere supported by strong social forces, that religions tend to have strong views about the morality of sex and contraception, and that the great majority of people in most countries are not aware of population growth and are indifferent to its implications. Given considerations such as these, one can begin to appreciate that a decision to adopt an antinatalist policy and to implement it with action programs may require a considerable degree of political courage. Yet such decisions do get made. Can it be that birth control is not as controversial an area as it has been thought to be? Are such decisions easier in some political systems than in others? How have they affected political fortunes? How do political leaders calculate possible gains and losses when considering population decisions? What types of information are taken into account in such calculations? Whose advice is sought and believed? How does population come to be a legitimate concern of government? What is the relation of political to technical considerations in decision making? (India has not yet adopted the oral contraceptive for mass use; Malaysia relies on it almost exclusively. Decisions to push or not push sterilizations may rest on political considerations. Abortion may be an excellent birth control procedure from a technical point of view but not tried in a given country because of political concerns.)

The Development of National Commitment—Political Will. Among the twenty-five or so countries that have explicit national policies and active government programs there is probably not one in which political commitment is sufficiently strong or sufficiently widespread to provide an effort consonant with the magnitude of the task of changing the reproductive behavior of a substantial segment of the population. If voluntary birth control is to have any chance of making a significant difference in growth rates in the time periods specified in national policies, population planning will have to have strong and continuing interest and support from the highest levels of political leadership. This it does not yet have. Nearly everywhere family planning tends to be defined as a health matter, and, typically, responsibility for promoting birth control and providing service is handed over to the health ministry, which is usually a low prestige agency already understaffed, overworked, underfinanced, and badly managed. In India, which has had a problem of almost unimaginable complexity and which has been officially concerned with population planning since 1952, the prime minister rarely mentions the topic in public statements, and there is no high government or political leader who can be identified as a champion for the national effort. The former president of Pakistan was deeply interested and kept in close touch with program developments in his country, but there have been doubts about the strength of commitment of the new government, although substantially increased funds have been made available for the plan period beginning this year. President Suharto has been a firm supporter of the developing program in Indonesia, and indeed a rapid change from the policies of his predecessor may be largely due to his interest and influence; but it is too soon to judge how vigorous the program is going to be. President Marcos in the Philippines was a prime mover in the events leading to the development of a policy and a program design for his country, but here too both are too new for any judgment to be made about how energetic and effective national efforts are likely to be. In Malaysia the prior interest of the minister of agriculture (now minister of commerce and industry and chairman of the National Family Planning Board), along with that of the minister of finance, were potent influences in getting the national program a semiautonomous status independent of any ministry but attached for administrative purposes to the powerful prime minister's department. In Ghana, initial impetus for a policy came from the former commissioner of economic affairs, and the program is administratively located in the high prestige Ministry of Finance. In most countries with policies, there is somebody reasonably high in government ·who has contributed to the adoption of the policy and to the establishment and continuation of programs, but rarely, if ever, is there a commitment in depth that would assure program vigor and the energetic pursuit of results.

The priority given to family planning is reflected in the budget allocations made for it. Of sixteen countries for which the Population Council has compiled budget information, three have allocated less than 1¢ per capita annually in recent years; six between 1¢ and 5¢; five from 6¢ to 10¢; and two over 10¢, one being India which is budgeting 15¢ annually for the fourth plan period, 1969-74. Viewed as proportions of total government budgets, the figures are even more revealing. Of twelve countries for which information is readily available, ten allocate less than 1/4 of 1 percent for family planning; one budgets 9/10s of 1 percent; and only one assigns a full 1 percent to this field.

A part of the task of government population planning programs is to bring about a voluntary change in the reproductive behavior of a substantial proportion of the national population. If they can succeed at all, it can only be through vigorous, sustained efforts, strongly and continuously endorsed and monitored by high level political leaders. In countries containing nearly three-fourths of the population of the developing world, enough support has been mustered to formulate and adopt policies and programs. But the depth and the range of commitment at the top is not yet sufficient for the long haul. Governments have approached population issues with a curious balance of boldness and timidity. To analyze how that balance comes about and to indicate how it might be altered is, I believe, a most important job for political science.

The Organization and Location of National Family Planning Programs. There are almost as many different forms of organization of government family planning programs as there are programs. Taiwan's program ran along for nearly ten years under an ostensibly private association whose directing members were largely government employees, before the government openly assumed responsibility in 1968. Korea, Costa Rica, and Kenya are operating programs with varying mixtures of government and private association responsibility. In Colombia, an association of schools of medicine took the lead in tooling up and planning for family planning and now shares the stage with a vigorous private association and some hesitant efforts by the Ministry of Health. In India, where the states are responsible for program operations and the central government for policy and funding, the federal system has led to serious problems of planning, program coordination, and evaluation. The Pakistan program is decentralized, with considerable autonomy for provinces and districts. Prior to 1965 this program was operated from the health ministry. More recently the principal directing body has been the National Family Planning Council, but there seems to be a rising swell of opinion that family planning should be reunited with health services. Malaysia, Ghana, and Indonesia have organizational patterns that permit representation on the governing bodies of private and industrial interests, religious bodies, and a number of ministries including health, education, social welfare, and information.

How a program is organized and where in the governmental structure it is located reflect how the program is conceived and determine how it operates. Location in the Ministry of Health generally implies a conservative approach in which family planning is offered through clinics and largely, if not exclusively, by health personnel. Overall direction by multiinterest *ad hoc* bodies administratively connected to high prestige ministries usually results in a greater emphasis on program components supplementary to service, such as education-information, training, and evaluation.

Organization and location probably *do* make a difference in the way a program is supported and how it performs. And decisions about the structure and location—both initially and in relation to subsequent modifications—are made in light of political as well as administrative considerations. I suspect that not much is known definitely about the political context in which such decisions are taken and the political forces that shape them.

National vs. Local Responsibility. Family planning programs generally tend to follow the broad pattern of organization and distribution of responsibility of other government activities. Small countries can operate with a high degree of central control; larger ones, e.g., India, Pakistan, U.A.R., Indonesia, must give considerable responsibility to regions, provinces, districts, and smaller units. The flow of power, influence, resources, and information through these complex systems is critical for staff performance and program accomplishment. They are not to any extent being studied. Perhaps they should be.

Population Growth and Distribution in Relation to Political Representation. The political science implications of this one should be obvious. In this country the problem arises in connection with reapportionment of legislative seats and with fears about the results of differential reproduction among socioeconomic and ethnic groups. The two-way relationship between political and demographic factors is especially apparent in this area. Political decisions can be a factor in both growth rates and distribution processes, and these in turn have political consequences. Our current policy on immigration, which accounts for a substantial proportion of the annual population increase, surely reflects political calculations about local preferences for or against one or another ethnic group. In African nations where tribal influences are strong in government, considerations of how one or another group might respond to family planning services and what the consequences might be for the political balance are rarely absent from the decision-making process. In countries like Malaysia where ethnic tensions are higher and population proportions reasonably close, a national family planning program must follow a narrow line and be certain that its offerings are made to and accepted by about the same proportion of all major groups.

Political and Legal Aspects of Abortion, Sterilization, and Contraceptives. In this country, general and political attitudes towards abortion are rapidly changing along with its legal status in a number of states. How did this happen, and what are its implications for similar change in other countries? Abortion has long been legal in Japan and Eastern Europe, and the experience of Rumania a year or two ago when the birth rate practically doubled following a shift in policy relating to abortion demonstrates what an important influence it can have on population growth. In the developing world Singapore has legalized abortion, and the Indian government is presently considering a bill that would liberalize its policy. In Latin America, however, such governmental involvement in family planning as exists tends to be justified in terms of its presumed effect on the number of illegal abortions. Contraception, sterilization, and abortion are necessary means to birth control at the micro level and to population stabilization at the macro level. But almost everywhere these are hedged about by legal, religious, and normative influences that limit their use and utility. What has happened here recently indicates that these influences can change—or be changed?—rapidly. What is necessary for such change, and how it can be initiated and stimulated in countries with serious population problems are matters that we need to know much more about.

Population Implications of Tax and Welfare Programs. It is plausible that tax and welfare policies have demographic effects, even though they may be hard to demonstrate. There are those who believe that a lack of social security provisions is an important influence in the continuing high fertility in developing countries, and the governments of Ghana and Singapore have enough confidence in the relationship of welfare and fertility that they are reducing maternity and children's allowances with the expectation that there may be effects on fertility. For the most part any effects that have occurred heretofore have been largely unintended and unnoticed, but with interest increasing in the broad and vague area that has been called "beyond family planning," the possibilities of manipulating tax and welfare arrangements to achieve a planned antinatalist effect are being mentioned. This is one of the areas that is specifically listed as appropriate for study in the program in support of social science and legal research on population policy recently announced jointly by the Ford and Rockefeller Foundations.

The Political Influence of Religious Groups in Population Decisions. This is an area of special significance in Latin America where relations between church and state seem to be especially influential, and where official Catholic disapproval of "artificial" methods of contraception has undoubtedly influenced political events. It is also an issue of some significance in a number of Muslim areas where, although national and international religious leaders generally approve of birth control, influential local leaders tend to be more conservative. In some countries—e.g., Malaysia and Indonesia—religious bodies are officially represented on the governing councils of national family planning programs. In others—as in the United States in relation to issues of sterilization and abortion—religious opinion is a significant factor in political discussion and decision.

Relations Between Government and Private Organizations in Population Matters. A not uncommon sequence of events is for population issues to be first discussed and services first provided by associations of citizens acting in their private capacity. When interest has sufficiently expanded and when (as a cynic might view it) family planning has been shown to be politically safe, governments begin first to allow their facilities to be used by private groups and later to take over leadership and responsibility for program continuation and expansion. Although a frequent objective of the private group is to involve the government and obtain its support, success brings problems that have jurisdictional and power components, and the transition from private to government leadership is not always entirely happy or harmonious. There are important and useful roles both for government and private initiative in family planning, but sometimes accommodation is difficult to achieve, and rarely is there optimal cooperation and the most effective use of the talents and resources of both.

Freedom and Coercion in Family Planning. This is a lively issue that is likely to be around for a while and to grow even more lively as time passes and population pressures become more apparent. Opinions tend to be highly polarized. For the purist exponent of absolute individual freedom in the matter of reproduction, even mild persuasion can be defined as intolerable coercion; for the extreme advocate of the need for population stabilization, societal needs justify, if they do not demand, curbs on individual reproduction. One justification for liberalizing access to contraception and abortion has been the argument that reproduction is a basic human right to be exercised by each couple in accordance with private and personal preference. It is this right that world leaders' statements promulgated by the United Nations have affirmed. And some nations—Ghana would be an example—have cited this right to justify partially governmental family planning activity. (The argument is that governments must provide information and service because those who are ignorant or who do not have access to the means of birth control do not have freedom of choice). Affirmation of reproduction as a basic individual right is something that both capitalist and communist nations can agree on, and it is this that permits the countries of Eastern Europe to maintain birth rates under 20 per 1000 while insisting that they have no population policy or program. There are many shades of opinion about whether or at what point incentives payments for using contraception or otherwise avoiding pregnancy constitute coercion. Surveys taken in many countries around the world show that almost invariably the verbal expression of family size ideals exceeds the number of children required for population stabilization. Such ideals, of course, are subject to change, and there will be, as populations grow, pressures to revise them downward. But in many places and for a fairly long time, birth rates are likely to remain substantially higher than death rates, and the difference may, in time, sharpen and intensify the issue of reproductive freedom vs. coercion to limit childbearing.

The Politics of Resettlement. People who view the population problem in terms of density point out that there is a lot of empty space still available for people to fill. Others agree but argue that it is empty because people can't or don't want to live there. The population of Kenya is largely concentrated in a relatively narrow band running from Kisumu to Mombasa, and the northern part of the country is practically empty. Brazilian leaders think of their vast northwestern areas and worry that if Brazilians don't quickly multiply and fill these spaces other land hungry peoples will. Americans leave the reasonably attractive middle spaces of their country and huddle together in sprawling clusters along the eastern and western coasts. And Indonesia, with some 3,000 islands, finds more than half its population crowded on Java. The dream that people can be resettled on empty lands is a durable one and one that receives confirmatory support in history. Migration has been a massive phenomenon at times in the past, but the opportunities are no longer abundant, and, in any case, most of the large migrations of the past were spontaneous rather than organized, much like the rural to urban movement that goes on in many countries today. That they were spontaneous does not mean, of course, that they were not influenced by government policies. Several countries have engaged in resettlement projects in an effort to distribute population more evenly, but in the main the projects have not been successful. The logistic problems of supplying and transporting even modest numbers of people are formidable, the capital requirements are larger than many developing nations can readily afford, and the political problems of recruitment and selection are difficult. As population pressures grow, however, as in Indonesia for example, distant pastures may come to look more attractive, and resettlement schemes may be revitalized. Should this happen, governments will need to devise new policies and arrangements to make empty areas more attractive, so that people will want to go there, or be faced with the politically unattractive prospect of selecting people to be moved.

Immigration Policy. Immigration policy, of course, serves political ends and is determined by political processes. Perhaps to some extent such policies also reflect demographic realities. There is some indication that Mauritius intends to handle the problem of high growth by exporting people. Whether there will be places willing to accept such emigrants indefinitely is questionable. The general tendency of governments seems to be in the direction of closing down opportunities for immigration, although certain countries of Europe claim a need for workers. The combination of growing populations, more restrictive migration policies, and increasing visibility of differences between more affluent and less affluent countries could generate explosive political tensions, both domestic and international.

National Sovereignty and Population Growth. Population growth is an internal matter. Each nation and each government decides for itself what its population policy will be. But no nation can any longer afford to ignore its own population trends or to be indifferent to the choices its neighbors make. The sources of population growth are localized within national boundaries, but in a real sense population growth constitutes a problem of regions and of the world. How national sovereignty and international concern and responsibility in population matters can be satisfactorily reconciled is a political problem as important as it is complex.

Politics of International Collaboration in Population Planning. For several years a number of governments (and a few private agencies) have been offering bilateral assistance in population planning. Such assistance is presumably politically neutral (and much of it, in fact, may be), but it also serves political purposes, both domestically and internationally, both for the donor and the recipient countries and presumably has political consequences for both. To a large extent aid for population planning may be no different from any other development assistance, but perhaps this is an area in which motives are more easily doubted and in which mistakes of either omission or commission could have more significant political repercussions.

Very recently, after several years of hesitation, the United Nations and its member organizations have begun moving to provide population planning assistance. In this effort political and technical considerations compete in interesting ways that should attract the attention of some political scientists, and the political maneuvering that goes on within and among agencies is also worthy of notice and study.

The Governing of Large Countries. There are seven countries in the world with populations over 100 million each (Brazil will soon join the club) and a combined population of over two billion—nearly 60 percent of total world population. Are there any special problems that arise in the attempt to govern countries such as these? Does size alone make the difference? Are political processes different from those of smaller countries? Are there inevitable consequences for individuality and personal freedom? Does large size speed up or retard modernization? I don't know the questions to ask, but there must be differences in the problems of governing China and those of Iceland that somehow derive from differences in population size.

All of the problem areas that have been mentioned (as well as many more, and possibly more important ones, that have been omitted) are, I think, of significance to those concerned with action aspects of population programs and policy and with the broader and longer range issues of population planning. Almost everywhere population growth confronts us with issues and prospects that we cannot ignore and for which we have few precedents and no clear and reliable guides to action. Those who work in the field are frequently "flying blind" because the studies that would provide the knowledge they need have not been done.

The questions I have raised are perhaps not the right ones, but they are illustrative of the kinds of questions that trouble people in the field, and they relate to areas in which social science help is needed. The problems of population programs, as someone has said, are not technical or financial; they are administrative and political. The need for new political insights and techniques is no less urgent than the need for better contraceptives. It is no small matter to attempt to change behaviors and values that have persisted for millenia. It is going to require a great deal of effort.

Some of it, I hope, will be made by political scientists.

Note

1. Edwin D. Driver, "The Social Sciences and Population Policy: A Survey," unpublished report to the Ford Foundation, February, 1970.

2 The Scholar and Political Strategy: The Population Case

Peter Bachrach

Introduction

Seldom is a solution to a major social or economic problem developed that is both technically and politically feasible. Keynesian fiscal policies and the Marshall Plan have been the rare breakthroughs in this respect during the past several decades. On the current horizon there appears to be no set of technical and political solutions to the problems of environmental pollution, urban decay, bureaucratic oligarchy, and overpopulation, to name but a few of the major problems that confront society. One oversight that has impeded the social scientist in his struggle to solve such critical issues has been, in my view, an insufficient attention to the phenomenon of political power.

The social scientist tends to err in one of two ways: either he is disposed in an incremental fashion to tailor his proposal, despite its deficiencies, to accommodate existing political realities; or, in the posture of the uncompromising scholar, he ignores the existing political realities in the course of his defense of the social and structural changes necessary to facilitate a proposed solution. In both cases the problem of power is essentially ignored.

The incrementalist assumes that the existing distribution of power, at least in the short run, is fixed and immutable; that since constraints are given and constant, the determination of correct political strategy presents little difficulty. The problem of strategy is almost nonexistent for the uncompromising scholar since he tends to assume that public exposure of the justification for social change—as a necessary means for solving a major problem—is in itself a powerful force for bringing about a prescribed change. Whether it is a sufficient force is not, as he views it, his concern. On occasion he will find it comforting to conclude his study along the lines that "the analysis of the issues and the formulation of goals are a necessary first step in marshalling a commitment to act."[1]

Apart from the substantive aspects of a public policy question, neither type of analyst seriously considers the formulation of the issue and the nature of the recommended solution as a *means* to generate and marshall commitment, public support, and power resources of potential or existing groups that, if properly motivated, would be instrumental in bringing about sufficient change in the distribution of power to secure the adoption of a meaningful government policy.

A strategy of this kind underscores the necessity to link a public policy issue and its proposed solution with the interests and goals of private groups. The objective of such a linkage is, on the one hand, to enhance the groups' public image and legitimacy, thereby increasing their power and influence; and on the other, to politically activate them in support of the public policy proposal.

The now famous phrase "maximum feasible participation" had this effect, although the framers of the Economic Opportunity Act did not anticipate it. It served to legitimize the demands of the poor for a share in the decision-making process in the antipoverty programs. In fact, the phrase soon developed into a forceful ideological justification for the poor and their leaders to take control of the funds and policymaking of various local projects. Although the combined power of city halls and the Republican Administration has succeeded in curtailing the activities of neighborhood organizations, what might be called the ideology of participation has been and still is a significant force in reordering the power distribution in the cities.[2]

Another strategy available to the scholar in a public policy area is to formulate issues, dicta, and recommendations as a means to provoke public controversy. Here the objective is to expand the scope of the conflict and deepen public concern in the issue in an effort to build a strong alignment of forces in support of meaningful action.[3] Whether Mayor Lindsay had this strategy in mind when he insisted that the Kerner Report include the sentence, "Our nation is moving toward two societies, one black, one white—separate and unequal"[4] is a matter of conjecture. Nevertheless, it was a plausible and justifiable strategy at a time when the country was stalled on an important issue that required bold and imaginative action.

True, the social scientist has become more and more interested in the study of political strategy and in utilizing game theory, simulation, and computer science in this pursuit. But his focus is usually upon how men of affairs—the statesman, the politician, the bureaucrat, the militant leader—should act to maximize their gains or minimize their losses rather than on what strategy the scholar should adopt when his scholarship and a public policy issue intertwine.

Of course the scholar's legitimate concern is to seek truth, not to gain power. But this begs the question of the relationship between truth and power as it pertains to his scholarship. Is an analysis of public policy "true" if it ignores the problem of power as it relates to bridging the gap between thought and action? In other words, should the scholar in his research of a public policy issue confine himself to the area of what exists and what ought to be, and thus ignore political strategy, the area of what can be?

Judging from the evidence of scholarly output, the overwhelming majority of scholars would reply to this question affirmatively.[5] I find this answer unacceptable on two grounds. First, abstaining from analysis of political strategy as it relates to a policy proposal does not preclude the intrusion of implicit or unexamined assumptions about power that may well affect the entire substantive analysis and which under scrutiny might be shown to be invalid. Second, I do not understand how a scholar in a public policy field can avoid accepting, explicitly or implicitly, a pragmatic view of truth; that is, from regarding the soundness of policy proposals in terms, among other criteria, of whether their transformation into practice is politically possible. Viewed in this way, truth can no longer be separated from power, nor is thought in a realm apart from action. For the analyst of public policy, therefore, to neglect to carefully examine political strategy as an integral part of his problem is to fail his responsibility as a scholar.

I am aware that this line of argument can be misinterpreted. I do not mean to suggest that the responsible scholar, in the manner of the Machiavellian activist, should bend every effort to gain public acceptance and adoption of the policy that he favors. Among other objections to this position, there is no assurance that he has a corner on the truth—that his policy preference is invariably an enlightened one and therefore should be adopted. As a scholar his legitimate concern is not whether the policy position he develops and supports is ultimately adopted; it is rather whether it is seriously considered by the public and by decision makers. It is owing to this latter concern that he has a responsibility to try to enlarge the scope of controversy so as to include his policy proposal, which he obviously believes is worthy of serious public consideration.

The following brief analysis of the controversy among scholars concerned with overpopulation highlights the problem of the adequacy with which policy issues are dealt at the level of the scholar.

The Controversy

An overwhelming majority of demographers and social scientists believe that a lower rate of world population growth is an imperative.[6] But there is sharp disagreement on what constitutes (1) an adequate decline in the birth rate, and (2) effective and proper means to achieve this decline. Proponents of family planning programs—which are now sponsored by the federal government at home and overseas in more than thirty countries—stand firmly on the principle of individual freedom of choice; that "Women everywhere need reproduce only if and when they choose."[7] According to this view, the goal must exclusively be focused upon the prevention of unwanted babies, not in restricting the number of children parents may wish to have. Critics of this position argue that family planning is not population control; that under present conditions the number of children couples want is in excess of the number required to achieve population stability. Individual free choice to procreate must therefore be limited to assure this and future generations the opportunity to enjoy lives free from overcrowding, hunger, and pollution.[8]

Shifting the argument to a more practical plane, defenders of family planning point out that "given the realities"—to use Bernard Berelson's phrase[9]—the on-going program has been eminently successful; that it has strong support in Congress and in an increasing number of developing nations; and that its promotion of birth control education and dispersal of contraceptives has had a significant effect upon population growth.[10] The thrust of their argument is clear—that the critics of family planning are performing a disservice to the cause of population stability; that ranks should be closed in support of the present policy. In this vein a recent AID report stated:

Because the extent of availability of family planning information and means is now usually a dominant determinant in the complex of forces influencing reproductive behavior, no definitive studies nor final judgments of additional measures which may ultimately be needed to achieve a desired rate of population growth can be made in advance of the full extension of family planning services.[11]

In effect, the report strongly advises that family planning should preempt the field of population research and policy formulation, at least during the foreseeable future. The success of family planning in Taiwan and South Korea is usually cited in support of this stand. Indeed in both countries, especially in Taiwan, family planning programs have been widely accepted, and the rate of population growth has markedly declined. The critics, however, have not been impressed by the Taiwanese experience. Although they do not deny that family planning was a factor in bringing about the decline, they point out that, as in the case of Japan, the decline followed the rapid industrialization of the country. But this point aside, the Taiwanese experience, as they see it, reflects the basic defect of the family planning approach. For in spite of its apparent success, the lower birth rate achieved there will nevertheless be sufficiently robust to double the population in forty-one years.[12] In light of this kind of evidence the population control advocates persist in maintaining that the near term goal must be a population growth rate approaching zero, rather than the more modest objective of a decline in population growth.

In rejecting the latter goal, critics of family planning also reject complete reliance on birth control education and improved contraceptive technology to solve the problem. In addition to advocating the adoption of antinatalist policies by public authorities, these critics emphasize the need to change the socialization process as it relates to family size.[13] It is especially contended that the institutions and values that motivate parents in developing countries to bear more children than are desirable from the standpoint of the public interest must be changed. This view is based, as I have indicated, on the statistical findings, which are generally accepted by demographers, that the prevention of unwanted children by widespread use of improved contraception and free abortions would not result in a sufficient reduction in the birth rate to meet a population policy goal of zero growth.[14] To meet this goal, it is argued, radical social change is absolutely necessary in most developing nations as a prerequisite to the rapid industrialization and changing socialization patterns that would foster widespread private desire to avoid large families.[15]

The dispute between the defenders of family planning and their critics touches a fundamental issue that underlies controversy on most major public policy questions: should policy objectives be on altering individual behavior within the constraints of existing social and political structures, or should policy be designed to change the social and political structures as a means of changing individual attitudes and behavior?[16] Given this choice, the position the policy maker adopts depends, among other considerations, on his disposition toward power. And, as I have argued, this question cannot be avoided by scholars whose findings and recommendations are essential inputs in the policy process. An interesting example of the first attitude toward power is contained in a letter by the Committee on Population of the National Academy of Sciences published in *Science*. In commenting on an article critical of family planning by Professor Kingsley Davis, the prestigious committee wrote:

A zero rate of population growth may be essential in the long run, but as a goal within the time horizon of current policy it has *little support* in either the developing or the developed world, certainly not among governments. Before any action in this direction is taken, it will be necessary to develop some consensus in support of the goal itself. . . . Programs of social change must operate within the framework of *existing values* and few governments are yet prepared to adopt stringent economic or social means to bring down birth rates.[17] (Emphasis added.)

It is interesting to note that the committee, at the outset, rejected both zero growth as a goal for the near term and social change as a means to achieve it, not on substantive grounds, but solely on the basis of power considerations. Certainly I do not find fault with the group for taking power into account. But the naive apparently hasty manner in which it considered the matter is somewhat disconcerting. Admittedly, a political strategy built upon consensus cannot be rejected out of hand. Is it not somewhat unrealistic, however, to believe that a political consensus can be developed in support of a goal that requires radical social change? I cannot think of a single instance in history when this has occurred. Because of its untenable position on this issue, the committee has exposed itself to the charge that it used power considerations as a cover to reject substantive recommendations that it could not or did not wish to consider on their merits.[18]

The letter also raises a serious ethical question, namely, the dubious propriety of a scientific committee's attempting to discourage further debate—as well as further research and investigation—on an extremely important and unresolved issue for other than substantive reasons. The letter, signed by leading authorities in the field and under the aegis of the top scientific organization in the country, could have had no other effect. The scientists were clearly exercising power by the nondecision-making route.[19] For in proclaiming that it must wait for a consensus before adopting zero growth as the population objective, the thrust of the committee's letter strengthened the already dominant position of family planning. As Professor Davis stated in his reply to the letter, the committee's support of "current population policies provides an escape from consideration of the painful social and economic changes necessary to achieve fertility control."[20]

By virtue of its "chilling effect" on future debate and research on this issue within the scientific community, the letter will have the further undesirable effect of decreasing the exposure of policy makers to relevant considerations and options that might influence their deliberations and the formulation of public policy. It is expected that within the policy process bureaucratic heads and political elites will inevitably engage in nondecision making. It would appear contrary to the spirit of scientific inquiry, however, for scholars to exercise power in this way.

It would be naive to think that power considerations could be extricated from substantive policy questions on any level of decision making. Scholars whose work is closely related to public policy issues will continue, as they should, to exercise power. My plea is that if they were more knowledgeable in its uses and implications, they would exercise it properly—that is, not to inhibit debate but to expand and invigorate it.

Scholars who favor population control have shown themselves to be no more sophisticated in the handling of power. Inevitably the experts of this persuasion advocate the adoption and enforcement by public authorities of strong antinatalist measures. For example, in order to achieve the goal of zero growth in the United States they propose an increase in the minimum age for marriage; a baby licensing system; various tax schemes that would penalize excess reproduction and benefit childless marriages and small families; compulsory sterilization after the birth of the n-th child; inclusion of antinatalist educational materials in the public school systems; compulsory abortion requirements; and similar measures.[21]

Since proposals such as these squarely repudiate the principle of individual freedom to procreate—a "right" deeply enmeshed in the value structure of the nation and proclaimed by the president as an irrevocable principle[22]—it is some wonder that their proponents are able to take them seriously. They are indeed persuaded that adoption of such laws is essential to the national interest and that, therefore, obsolete moral precepts—although widely held—must be relinquished in the interest of the country's health and well-being.

Morally and philosophically the argument may be persuasive, but viewed politically it is unimpressive. The argument fails to consider the disparity that frequently occurs in American politics between what might be called national concerns and political issues. A tragedy of American political life is that rarely, short of national crisis, does a national concern become a political issue. Thus, an apathetic political reception is the current fate of policy proposals designed to achieve population stability. Even if the proposals were ideologically compatible with existing pronatalist values and institutions, it is unlikely that they would attract sufficient public interest and support to be converted into a political issue. Their lack of conversion power is chiefly due to the fact that benefits of population control would be widely and indirectly distributed and would not be forthcoming for a considerable period of time.

I do not mean to suggest that population control in the United States is necessarily a goal that is politically impossible to attain. But if a serious effort is to be made in this direction, a strategy must be employed that avoids a frontal attack upon entrenched moral beliefs and principles. And equally important, it must be a strategy that demonstrates that policy proposals designed to achieve the national interest will also benefit the private interests of partisan organizations. The ultimate objective of such a linkage is to generate enough power to transform a national concern into a political issue—and, after that, a political issue into public policy.

Initially the purpose of the connection is to construct a mutuality of interests between the public good and the desires of private groups in order to spur political activity by the latter in support of the former. Hopefully as private groups become politically activated, their conception of their interests will broaden as they perceive that their individual well-being is inextricably linked to the public well-being.[23] And as they acquire greater status and respectability as spokesmen for a public cause, their power and influence are bound to increase. Thus the strategy is both to activate and to build a power base in support of a public issue. It is a common occurrence for the "national interest" to be invoked by someone to prevent action that may be detrimental to his vested interest.[24] When applicable, it should be invoked the other way around.

For example, this strategy could now be successfully used to mobilize women's liberation organizations in support of the goal of population control. The interest of supporters of population control would be significantly served if they used their power to aid women's liberation groups to realize one of their goals—compelling the government to enforce its policy providing for equal education and economic opportunities for women—for the antinatalist sentiment that would be generated by such an enforcement would be profound. As job and career opportunities become a reality—for low as well as middle-class women—the incentive to bear and care for large families would undoubtedly decline. And as women acquired a foothold in the educational systems, their changing aspirations, values, and power resources could well lead to a further attack against pronatalist institutions. The weakening of these institutions would inevitably enhance the possibility of attaining population stability.

The likelihood that women's liberation organizations, which are currently fractionalized and weak, could be fused and unified by an identity of interest with a national goal is of course a matter of conjecture. It is, however, a strategy worth considering.

It is true that often there are situations in which no strategy can be effective in changing the existing distribution of power. However, this does not lessen the force of my argument that it is intellectually indefensible for scholars to ignore or inadequately investigate the problem of power in relation to substantive policy issues. For there is always the possibility that, owing to the dynamics of other forces at work, the present configuration of power will significantly change. To ignore this contingency, to assume that present "political realities" will persist over time, is to be unprepared when change actually occurs. Rather than exploiting changing conditions for the adoption of improved and innovative policies, it is to invite policy formation by inertia. Until recently, for instance, supporters of family planning disapproved on ethical grounds of abortions as a means of limiting population growth. In fact, one of the arguments used in favor of family planning, both as practiced overseas and at home, was that it effectively eliminated the need for abortions. It was not until substantial political pressure for more permissive abortion laws in this country developed that family planning policy changed in conformity with this trend.

By adhering to a rigid and doctrinaire line that is inattentive to possible social and political change, the uncompromising scholar makes himself incapable, when change actually occurs, of contributing toward the conversion of his policy preferences into public policy. In the absence of a political constituency, his position remains sterile. On the other hand, in subscribing to a static concept of power, the incrementally-inclined scholar is caught off guard by the necessity to adjust his policy position to changing "political realities." Neither approach is conducive to the achievement of essential national goals.

Notes

1. For example, see the concluding statement in Peter Morrison, "The Rationale for a Policy on Population Distribution" (Santa Monica: Rand Corporation, 1970), p. 17.

2. See, for example, P. Bachrach and M. Baratz, *Power and Poverty* (New York: Oxford University Press, 1970); J. May, "Politics of Growth versus the Politics of Redistribution," in George Frederickson (ed.), *Citizen Participation* (forthcoming); M. Gittel, *Participants and Participation* (New York: Praeger, 1967); F. Riessman and A. Gartner, "Community Control and Radical Social Change," *Social Policy* (May-June 1970), pp. 52-56; and P. Green, "Decentralization, Community Control, and Revolution," in P. Green and S. Levinson (eds.), *Power and Community* (New York: Pantheon Books, 1970).

3. E.E. Schattschneider, *The Semisovereign People* (New York: Holt, Rinehart, 1960), pp. 1-47.

4. *Report of the National Advisory Commission on Civil Disorders* (New York: Bantam Books, 1968), p. 1.

5. For example, a leading authority on the population problem wrote, "For clear thinking about population policy, the question of effectiveness must be separated from that of acceptability." Reply letter to "Family Planning and Other Population Controls," letter by members of the Committee on Population, National Academy of Sciences, *Science* (February 23, 1968), p. 828. For a general discussion, see C. Wright Mills, *Sociological Imagination* (New York: Oxford University Press, 1959).

6. B. Berelson, "National Family Planning Programs: Where We Stand," *Studies in Family Planning*, no. 39, Supplement (New York: Population Council, March, 1969). The 1970 Nobel Peace Prize winner, Dr. Norman Borlaug, asserted, "If the world population continues to increase at the same rate, we will destroy the species." *New York Times*, 22 October 1970, p. 18.

7. R.T. Ravenholt and J.J. Speidel, "Prostaglandins in Family Planning Strategy" (Washington, D.C.: Agency for International Development, September, 1970), p. 2.

8. See J. Blake, "Population Policy for Americans: Is the Government Being Misled?" *Science* (May 2, 1969); K. Davis, "Population Policy: Will Current Programs Succeed?" *Science* (November 10, 1967); G. Hardin, "Parenthood: Right or Privilege?" *Science* (July 31, 1970).

9. Berelson (n. 5).

10. Berelson, "National Family Planning Programs: Where We Stand," *Science*, September 4, 1970.

11. Ravenholt (n. 7), p. 3.

12. Davis (n. 8).

13. See Blake and Davis (n. 8).

14. L. Bumpass and C. Westoff, "The 'Perfect Contraceptive' Population" *Science* (September 18, 1970).

15. See especially Davis (n. 8).

16. For a discussion of this point, see P. Marris and M. Rein, *Dilemmas of Social Reform* (New York: Atherton, 1967).

17. *Science*, February 23, 1968, p. 827.

18. In effect, this is what Davis accuses the committee of. See his reply, ibid.

19. For a discussion of this concept, see Bachrach and Baratz, *Power and Poverty* (n.2).

20. *Science*, February 23, 1968, pp. 828-29.

21. See J.J. Spengler, "Population Problem: In Search of a Solution," *Science*, December 5, 1969; P. Ehrlich, "Paying the Piper," *New Scientist*, no. 36, 1967; and S. Wayland, "Family Planning and the School Curriculum," in B. Berelson (ed.), *Family Planning and Population Programs* (Chicago: University of Chicago Press, 1966).

22. In his population message to Congress in July, 1969, President Nixon stated: "In no circumstances will the activities associated with our pursuit of this goal be allowed to infringe upon the religious convictions or personal wishes and

freedom of any individual, nor will they be allowed to impair the absolute right of all individuals to have such matters of conscience respected by public authorities." *New York Times*, 12 August 1970, p. 16.

23. This is a different route to the "general will" than Rousseau's, but it draws from the latter the basic insight that the interest of the community can only be obtained if "man, in considering himself, votes for all." *Social Contract*, book 1, chapter 4. This is fundamentally different from President Kennedy's famous dictum exhorting Americans to work for their country. It is not a question of altruism or good citizenship, but of self-identity with the general interest.

24. R.A. Bauer, "The Policy Process," in R.A. Bauer and K. Gergen (eds.), *The Study of Policy Formation* (New York: Free Press, 1968), p. 12.

3

Population Policies and the American Political System

Theodore J. Lowi

It is the fate of government to deal with many problems for which there are no acceptable solutions. Population growth may prove to be a case in point. Demographers can plot the curves and identify the correlates, but population pressure is at bottom a problem of political economy, and in this respect Malthus continues to have the last word.

Yet, even if there are few theoretic guidelines, future governments will probably experiment on a large scale with population growth policies. Modern man rejects being a mere creature of his environment. He often demands and rarely rejects authoritative decisions about how he, and his neighbor, shall live. One of the first distinctly modern philosophers, David Hume, put the case this way:

Two neighbors may agree to drain a meadow, which they possess in common: because it is easy for them to know each other's mind; and each must perceive, that the immediate consequence of his failing in his part, is the abandoning of the whole project. But it is very difficult, and indeed impossible, that a thousand persons should agree in any such action; . . . each seeks a pretext to free himself of the trouble and expense, and would lay the whole burden on others. Political society easily remedies both these inconveniences.[1]

If, as is probable, the future brings a significant expansion of government policies to control population growth, these policies could have a serious impact upon the political system. And this is possible even if the policies failed to make a dent in the population growth profile itself. The impact of population growth policies on the American political system could be particularly significant for at least three reasons. First, the population field is more vast than any domestic sphere into which the federal government has ever tried to introduce central controls. Second, many, if not most, of these policies would intrude into areas once defined as within the realm of civil liberties and beyond the reach of government power altogether. Third, without established theoretical guidelines the numbers and types of such policies could become quite large, and the costs of implementation and impact could be very high—and again, even if the actual impact of these policies on population growth itself were negligible.

If any political impacts of these policies can be foreseen, the time is more than ripe to identify them—and to plan accordingly. For, if we can identify patterns of impact on the political system, these patterns could serve as criteria for defining good policy without interfering at all with the right of the people to have population growth policies if the majority so wills. For example, if two alternative population policies appear to experts to have about the same probability of significant impact on the growth profile, and if one of the alternatives could be shown to be more favorable to the maintenance of open, democratic policy making, then that alternative ought to be preferred. Or, if two policies are about equally likely to fail, then one should be preferred to the other if it can be shown to produce more justice, however it be defined. Some policies, regardless of impact on society, may produce a more exciting polity, or a more flexible one. Some policies may produce more civic education than others. Some may be conducive to a stronger Congress or to stronger national parties. There may, in sum, be some side benefits for the political system on the way to the war on population pressure, and the greater the uncertainty regarding ultimate societal impacts, the greater should be the concern for the side benefits as guides to public policy.

This paper is concerned with those side benefits. The case for the desirability of population planning in the United States does not yet enjoy broad consensus. And the projected impact on society of each specific proposal for control of population growth remains at best unclear. Specialists in the various aspects of demography, biology, and medicine will continue to evaluate population programs from the standpoint of impact and acceptance. Evaluation of these same proposals should be taking place at the same time from the standpoint of their possible impact on the political system. If political science has any expertise to offer, it should include this kind of evaluation.

What is "Population Policy?"

Such an evaluation requires a proper definition of the problem—or perhaps a redefinition—from the point of view of the political scientist rather than the demographer, the biologist, or the physician. And from this point of view, the most problematic concept is not *population* or *control*. It is *policy*. A proper definition and explication of this concept will shed a great deal of light on the other concepts and, it is hoped, on the substantive problem itself. And at the outset this involves identifying what policy is *not*.

First, policy is not merely a statement of the problem. Documentation does not speak for itself. Clearly stated cases of overpopulation and well-supported arguments of cause and effect are not policies. And neither is an expression of sentiments about the problem a policy. To summarize these two points quite concretely, a *whereas* covering the problem and its causes, followed by a *therefore* stating, for example, that we need zero population growth is not a policy. At best it is an admission that a policy dealing with the problem at hand may be desirable.

Policy is also not an appropriation backing sentiment. At least, that is not what we shall be calling policy here. Statements of fact, coupled with expressions of sentiment, attached to an authorization for expenditure are the typical three sections of American public policies. But these actions merely enable others to take actions on behalf of policy makers. And what this means is that some real policies are being made by obscure officials down at lower levels of some specialized bureaucracy, or it means that some social movement has been bought off by being given the impression that serious actions are taking place, when typically no real actions are taking place at all.

If these are pseudopolicies, what, then, does a *real* policy look like? *A policy is a general statement by some governmental authority defining an intention to influence the behavior of citizens by use of positive and negative sanctions.* A policy can influence behavior by use of monetary inducements, as in the case of the so-called farm parity programs. Or a policy can seek to influence conduct by threat of punishment. A single decision, a specific issue, or a description of the activities of a public official all constitute the data by which we instruct ourselves about a policy. But these are not policies. A policy must possess the following three characteristics: (1) an official expression of intentions concerning desirable or undesirable conduct; (2) a provision for inducements, positive, or negative, or both; and (3) some provision of means for implementing the intentions and applying the sanctions.

In light of this, analytic clarity will be enhanced if we eliminate the notion of "population policy" altogether and concentrate instead upon population *policies*. Population *policy* usually signifies a broadly stated sentiment that, at best, encourages serious consideration of specific proposals for population policies. But if our concern is for assessing impacts, the focus ought to cut through to the clearest cases of probable future public actions that intend to be effective. A statute or decree enunciating zero population growth as a goal would be nothing but an expression of sentiment. Setting up a department or independent commission on population would also be a pseudo-policy until such time that the agency itself generated some real policies. It is necessary to look carefully at each activity and proposal, to identify intentions, to assess sanctions, and after that, to look toward likely impact—upon the relevant demographic rate, and, for the political scientist, upon the political system as it seeks to affect the population.

Once real policies have been defined, proper assessment requires still another distinction. Some governmental activities affect the population without intending to, while others can explicitly adopt population impact as the goal. War is, for example, an important policy of governments, and war has a profound effect on population size and composition. But it would be stretching a point to call the typical war a population policy. Other examples of population-relevant policies that are not actual population policies include expansion of hospital services, reduction of the price of wonder drugs, food stamp plans, improved sanitation and epidemiology in cities, development and dispensation of new vaccines, and so on. Except for war, most of these population-relevant governmental activities seem to have an upward effect on population growth rates. Expansion of new and serious policies aimed at reduction in population growth rates might therefore be at cross purposes with many population-relevant welfare policies. This could be a real dilemma in the future.

In contrast, and still more ironically, there are many policies, especially at the local level, that are coming to be seen as undesirable or downright unconstitutional. Examples include exclusive zoning; segregated public housing; and other housing, schooling, and service programs that maintain ghettos and slums. Yet, if, as is likely, these local programs are invalidated, there could be an upward tendency in population growth rates among the families who have most to gain by the elimination of those bad laws and programs.

These are factors and paradoxes that have to be taken into account in any serious effort to develop a plan for population growth. Modern medicine, technology, and enlightened welfare policies tend—by reducing death rates and even without affecting birth rates—to make population growth rates upwardly flexible and downwardly sluggish. This could be comparable to the effect of organized labor on wages. All of this suggests the extreme significance and the potential political divisiveness of any intentional population growth control policies, for the intentional policies must cut across important existing welfare and urban policies and affect the many and profound interests already tied to those policies.

The closer one gets to the serious and intended population growth policies, the more one sees these and other ramifications. To have a planned and measurable effect on population growth, most population policies must be aimed at birth rates, the more so as modern amenities keep pushing death rates, especially infant mortality, down. But such policies can hardly avoid class, ethnic, and racial bais. Even when equitably drafted and implemented, population control policies can be most burdensome among those least able to bear the burdens. To many, especially from an international perspective, population policies can be made to look like a white racist plot against the colored populations of the world.

This special problem of the real and symbolic biases in so many population policies can surely, with careful consideration, be softened, if not altogether eliminated. Nevertheless, the problem itself helps to identify and emphasize the one common and unavoidable characteristic of all real public policies, including population policies: *coercion*. This will turn out to be the most important analytic characteristic. One might quibble over fine points and special definitions, but it is wise to follow as a general rule the proposition that it is impossible to have a government policy without having coercion. Coercion can be remote and indirect, as in the case of government services where the recipient of those services need hardly be aware of the fact that the financing is based on a highly coercive revenue system. And coercion, as suggested before, can involve positive or negative sanctions, can be benevolent or malevolent, can coerce some in order to be of explicit assistance to others. But policy is no less coercive because there are different forms of it. This only means that governments have a choice among types of coercion, among types of persons to be coerced, and among the various sanctions to be employed. In fact, it is these very distinctions among types of coercion that will provide the basis for all the propositions about the different impacts than can be anticipated from the various efforts to control population growth rates.

A Scheme of Analysis

Classifying population policies, or any other policies, according to the type of coercion involved amounts to an attempt to define policies according to those elements most likely to have political implications. The possibility of being coerced or the prospect of coercing others must be highly motivating factors in political life; and if that is true, then a proper classification of policies in these terms could have a lot of predictive power in our effort to assess how these policies will shape political institutions and patterns in the decades to come.

To simplify matters as much as possible, let us substitute the word "statute" whenever the word "policy" crops up. In doing this, we give up a great deal of information about the policy in the real world. But we gain a great deal in clarity; and even from this partial and very formalized statement of policy in the statute, we can predict enough of the resultant political reality to provide a basis for judging the policy itself and determining whether it is one we would recommend adopting.

The predictive propositions we would like to be able to make can be indicated by the following questions:

1. Will the particular policy (statutory) effort favor executive power over legislative power?
2. Will the particular policy (statutory) effort be dominated by career bureaucrats, or will their activities be joined by nongovernmental specialists, opinion leaders, and groups; or will the effort be dominated by high-level officialdom?
3. Will the particular policy (statutory) effort enhance the power of congressional committees, or will the effort tend to accentuate the parliamentary powers on the floor of the House and the Senate?
4. Will the politics of the effort in question ground itself in interest groups or in social movements—or neither?
5. What kinds of policies seem most frequently to be associated with party politics, and, among these, which ones tend to encourage central and national parties as opposed to local parties?

Obviously there are other, more subtle behavior patterns that political scientists are interested in. But when a government is on the brink of committing itself to a vast new undertaking, it is most important to be able to anticipate gross developments in the large institutional aggregates.

Table 3-1 is an attempt to systematize the types of coercion available to governments as they seek to influence their environments. It simply translates earlier observations about coercion and its types into a more formal and exhaustive statement of logical possibilities.[2] The vertical dimension of the table suggests that, in a governmental context, coercion can be remote if the sanctions accompanying a given decision are mild or uncertain. Coercion can also be remote if it is indirect—as in the earlier illustration of a program based on services or subsidies where the coercion is displaced on to the general revenue system. When coercion is direct or immediate, it is usually quite easy to find in the statute.

The horizontal dimension is slightly less obvious, but no less important to the understanding of public policies. Some government decisions work by coming to bear specifically upon individual conduct. For example, there can be a general rule governing false and fraudulent advertising, but it is applicable to the conduct of individual advertisers. In strong contrast, some public policies seek to influence conduct not by direct application of coercive measures on the individual but rather by manipulating the environment of his conduct. For example, a minor change in the Federal Reserve discount rate can have a tremendous impact on my marginal propensity to investment, yet no government official need know of my existence.

In each of the four cells in table 3-1 there is a label for a type of public

Table 3-1
Types of Coercion and Types of Policy

| | Applicability of Coercion (Works through:) | |
	Individual Conduct	Environment of Conduct
Likelihood of Coercion: Remote	*Distributive* (e.g., 19th Century land policies, tariffs, subsidies)	*Constituent* (e.g., reapportionment, setting up a new agency, propaganda)
Immediate	*Regulative* (e.g., elimination of substandard goods, unfair competition, fraudulent advertising)	*Redistributive* (e.g., Federal Reserve controls of credit, progressive income tax, social security)

q

policy. It is not necessary to provide elaborate definitions of each, since the essential aspect of each definition is implied in the cross-tabulation of the two dimensions of coercion. Distributive policies are best illustrated by the nine-teenth-century land grant programs. Modern examples include the work of such agencies as the Extension Service, Soil Conservation Service, Weather Bureau, Office of Education, or Corps of Engineers which work strictly from the per-spective of benefits. One of the synonyms for this kind of policy is "patronage," not as a mere giving of jobs but in the generic sense of "to patronize."

Regulatory policies are also specific as regards individual conduct; but regula-tory policies are very different along the other dimension, for here the likelihood of coercion is quite immediate. In the regulatory statute one has no trouble finding the provision for sanctions. These sanctions can be inducements, as in the case of farm "parity" programs; or they can, more frequently, be punish-ments. But they can be found, and they are associated with certain conducts that the statute seeks to encourage or discourage.

A constituent policy, such as establishing the Office of Management and Budget or passing a reapportionment statute, may have profound effects on individual conduct; but the coerciveness of the government decision itself in either case follows from some basic change in the structure in which individuals operate. Or, the coerciveness may follow from decisions made by the Office of Management and Budget but not flowing *directly* from the statute setting it up. In contrast to this, a redistributive policy, such as the Federal Reserve rate mentioned above, or a basic change in the internal revenue structure, affects individuals through their environment; but unlike constituent policies, these are directly rather than indirectly coercive.

Table 3-2 attempts to capture a few of the political characteristics that a commonsense review of table 3-1 ought to generate. If the policy distinctions have any meaning at all, each category immediately suggests a regular and pre-dictable association with its own distinct political process. This is only to say in another way that if coercion comes in more than one form, so will politics.

Each of the characteristics of coercion seems to be associated with some fairly clear consequences for political behavior. For example, we know that historically log-rolling, localized parties were very much associated with the nineteenth-century federal government preference for subsidy, i.e., distributive policies.[3] But when the policies at issue were constituent, as in the nineteenth century when new states were admitted to the Union, a very different set of political characteristics prevailed. Party organizations dominated, but they were more nationalized, centralized, and ideological.[4] Distributive policies are likely to combine electoral and decentralizing political tendencies (the mixing of mar-ginal characteristics (1) and (3) on table 3-2) because the remoteness of coercion and the individualized focus allow each distributive decision to be made almost completely in isolation from other decisions. This is the essence of log-rolling, and a log-rolling politics is generally the most stable and usually out of public

Table 3-2
Types of Coercion and Characteristics of Arenas[a]

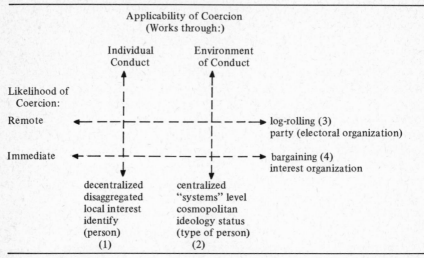

Applicability of Coercion
(Works through:)

Individual Conduct — Environment of Conduct

Likelihood of Coercion:

Remote ← log-rolling (3) / party (electoral organization)

Immediate ← bargaining (4) / interest organization

decentralized disaggregated local interest identify (person) (1)

centralized "systems" level cosmopolitan ideology status (type of person) (2)

[a]For more detailed characteristics of each arena—i.e., the sorts of things that would fill the cells above—see my "American Business, Public Policy, Case Studies and Political Theory," *World Politics*, July, 1964, Diagrammatic Summary, p. 713.

view. Constituent policies tend to produce mixtures of political characteristics (2) and (3) precisely because efforts to change the structure of conduct involve central and historical (i.e., ideological) considerations that cannot be so stable or so covert as the mixture of (1) and (3) characteristics. By the same pattern of reasoning, we can predict that political processes composed of (1) and (4) characteristics will tend to develop around regulatory policies, and that processes composed of mixtures of (2) and (4) characteristics will tend to develop around redistributive policies.

These have been the central hypotheses of a large-scale research project in policy processes which began in 1962. Although it would be overly burdensome to present the tests and methods here,[5] it might be useful to report a few of the findings that bear most clearly upon our present effort to make projections about the impact of population policies on political processes—i.e., findings that suggest patterns of institutional variation. For example, statistical analysis of the amending process reveals, as predicted, that distributive bills are dominated by congressional committees; regulative bills are dominated by the floor, with the executive being creatively involved; and redistributive bills are dominated by the executive, with a fairly pronounced role reserved for the open floor.[6] From a twenty-year analysis of roll call votes, it can further be shown, again as predicted, that the behavior of members of Congress in distributive issues is dominated by party relationships but that on redistributive issues, behavior tends to be ordered along nonparty, ideological lines. Legislative behavior on regulative issues is not ordered by any single factor at all; rather, it is here that coalitions tend to build virtually from bottom up for each issue.[7]

Finally, extensive reanalysis of seventeen major policy-making case studies produced confirming patterns in a variety of areas.[8] These detailed studies tended strongly to bear out statistical patterns and direct observations: The executive is the center of redistributive politics, the groupings tend to be very large and stable, and their relations are quite strongly ideological. Congress is at the center of regulatory politics, and it operates largely as a terrain where groups, through shifting coalitions, make policy by sharing interests. Congressional committees, alone or in combination with low-level administrative agencies, dominate the distributive policy process, using party and log rolling within party lines to get majority votes.

These distinctions will be pursued below. Their purpose here was to demonstrate the plausibility of the notion that policies determine politics, and that, therefore, the impact of policies on the political system can be predicted and planned for. Thus the projected impact of policies on politics can be developed as a criterion of policy choice, a criterion that does not have to await the long-range impact of a policy on the society.

Population Policies and their Politics

Evaluation of population policies has hardly begun in earnest in the United States. Ehrlich, for example, devotes more than 90 percent of his book[9] to an alarmist treatment of the problem calculated to produce a public opinion supportive of population planning. Late in the book, Ehrlich proposes several policies which, if seriously drafted and implemented, would very probably cut the growth rate. But as an enthusiast, he leaves the job of evaluation to others.

Among the many kinds of evaluation now beginning to take place, perhaps the most difficult and controversial are the socioeconomic and political. One of the pioneering efforts in this area is Nash's evaluation of population growth policies from two important political perspectives. He categorizes proposals according to the degree to which they clash with basic American political norms ("Lockean norms") and according to their potential for mass acceptance.[10] The present effort jumps off from there in an effort to determine whether these various policies have any lasting effect on political patterns and institutions. The four categories employed here are not based upon projected divisiveness, as are Nash's, yet since divisiveness and its long-range consequences ought to be predictable from categories that are based upon type of coercion, the Nash and the Lowi categories are not at all inconsistent or incommensurate. On the contrary, since Nash's distinctions are empirical, they can be subsumed by my nominalist-conceptual distinctions and operate in large part as confirmations of the power of public policies to predict political patterns.[11]

Distributive Policies

Examples of distributive population policies are: subsidies for research on birth control, etc.; subsidies for pharmaceutical houses to improve contraceptive chemicals and to reduce their prices; grants to wholesalers and retailers of contraceptives to encourage lower prices and more promotion; cash payments for women who accept intrauterine devices; subsidies for doctors and hospitals to encourage sterilization programs; expansion of clinics to provide guidance and promotion in this field.

These kinds of policies most resemble Nash's first category, the least divisive, the least violative of traditional values.[12] Consequently, they are the ones most likely to be adopted earliest and in largest number. Whatever conflict does develop can be displaced among many interests—a pattern that has generally been called log rolling. These programs, once enacted, tend to enjoy a kind of consensus because access to them can be universalized—anyone who objects to the benefits someone else is getting can be included. Perhaps with each expansion of access everyone already included gets a little less, but everyone can get something. The colorful term "porkbarrel" has developed to describe the programs in this category that dispense material benefits. But the word applies equally well to the service programs in this category.

The voluntaristic appearance of these programs, with such an attraction of potential consensus, or perhaps because of such an attraction, has at least two consequences worth serious assessment. First, the distributive approach could minimize the desired impact on population growth rates. Many people, especially in cultures and subcultures that set high value on large families or male heirs, will turn to these programs only after having their second son, even if this involves their third or fourth child. To guard against that kind of abuse or manipulation of the spirit of these programs, governments might then seek to interpose certain standards between the person and the services. Such statutes could be revised so that they are no longer merely permissive and enabling statutes. Sections could be added that limit the discretion of the administrators, so that services would be rendered or cash would be paid "only if" the seeker had fulfilled certain standards. But—as suggested by the paradigm—the imposition of standards of conduct changes the character and the politics of the programs in a fundamental way. The type of policy would have changed toward the regulatory quadrant, and the consensus politics would tend to be replaced by something more divisive.

The second consequence flows over time from the very type of consensus these programs can purchase. The "power structure" around distributive policies tends to be highly resistant to change. If subsidy and permissive service policies in the population field even faintly come to resemble their counterparts in other fields, where many studies have been made—such as natural resources, defense procurement, the traditional tariff, and agricultural extension—we should expect that control would come to rest a considerable distance from politically responsible levels and would tend to resist being recentralized if and when a change is desired. Local elites have many resources when it comes to resistance. These include the local administrators of the program, the congressmen whose reelection may be tied to the maintenance of these benefits, and the congressional committees or subcommittees which often come to be dominated by those whose most outstanding interest is in the maintenance of the program.[13]

It should further be emphasized how much all of the case studies of distributive policies discover that the committee or subcommittee system is the national center of distributive politics.[14] When Woodrow Wilson in 1886 complained that "Congressional government is committee government,"[15] he was actually describing the pre-twentieth-century Congress that dealt in almost nothing but distributive policies. Once the federal government began to take on modern—that is, regulatory and redistributive—tasks, the centers of national politics began to shift. But even now, on those numerous occasions when subsidy or porkbarrel policies are being adopted, the executive tends to be relegated to a lobby role at best, and the floor acts as a House of Commons; the Crown shifts according to whatever committee's distributive legislation is on the calendar.[16]

One might at first blush consider that these political results are a worthy price to pay in order to get going on a large scale in this new and controversial area. But the trouble is, once a commitment is made to the distributive pattern of public policy and takes on elements of distributive politics, the very agencies themselves may join in opposing later changes that may aim at making the whole program more effective. One good example of this is the vigor with which the Public Health Service avoided being shackled with the regulatory policies that flowed from their own findings and recommendations on the problems of air pollution.[17] Another example is the way in which the Office of Education has evaded responsibility for regulatory programs in the field of education standards or race discrimination in education.[18] Perhaps the most famous example is the Corps of Engineers and the way that agency has successfully avoided anything that breaks up their intimate relationship with the Public Works Committees of Congress, and the joint effort of the corps and the committes to avoid any outside planning criteria in the development of water control and navigation.[19]

None of the case studies is concerned with population policies. However, if the political patterns described here are only in a partial way repetitive whenever distributive policies prevail, it would seem wise to adopt these possibilities as criteria in any consideration of population policy proposals.

Constituent Policies

Included here are such policies as setting up a Department of Population Control, and setting up vigorous programs of education and propaganda in birth control. One of the big problems here of course is that many of these appeals are least effective where they are most needed. However, programs for effectiveness can be designed even for the least literate and for communities outside mass communication systems in the United States or abroad. Information on the availability and desirability of birth control devices and medications can be provided for and received and understood by people of all races, classes, and religions. Appeals on the basis of a better life for children, attacks on the need for a male heir, and revisions of public attitudes on abortion can reach all levels of all cultures, especially if the campaigns have government sponsorship and if appeals can be made on the basis of patriotism.

If such policies were adopted on a large scale, the short-run political consequences could be profound, even if their impact on population growth rates were not felt for a very long time. As Nash's second category suggests—and his examples of policies in this second category heavily overlap the constituent policy category[20]—constituent policies do not directly force people to do anything, and, thus, can be expected to be less intensely divisive and conflictive than policies that do directly coerce. However, a concerted effort to alert some people, and actually to change the values of many others, constitutes something of an assault on existing values and practices. The question is, therefore, not whether such policies will be divisive but how, and in what manner?

Almost so as to emphasize the divisiveness of constituent policies, proponents of population control policies are quite torn about whether an assault on traditional values will be divisive. Their response to the first systematic study of opinions on birth control suggest the degree of their concern as well as the probable character of the political pattern in this area of policy. Judith Blake's analysis of many opinion studies concluded that 29 percent of the non-Catholic wives in 1960 were against even such mild limitations as spacing pregnancies. Among lower income Catholic wives, 48 percent expressed opposition to birth control. Blake also reported that 79 percent of all wives of grade school education in the sample already used contraceptives to varying extents, and that many of the remaining 21 percent were younger women not using contraceptives because they wanted pregnancy.[21] A year later, Bumpass and Westoff reported what was in their estimation a strongly conflicting set of figures. They showed, for example, that almost 20 percent of recent births in the United States were "unwanted"; perhaps the proportion of "unwanted" births, they surmise, could have been greater among people in lower economic and education brackets and ethnic groups.[22]

All of these figures are soft and are susceptible to considerable manipulation by special pleaders on both sides of the population control issue. However, one line of argument seems supportable in both sets of studies. Appeals for family planning as a patriotic duty do constitute more than the putting of useful information before the public. It involves something of an assault on traditional values. Traditional values may not be held so strongly anymore, but the assault may indeed restore their strengths to many, while activating many others who have always been orthodox but passive on these matters. Moreover, if the appeals come to be seen as biased against special groups known to have large families, the possibilities for political divisiveness are not remote. And even as the proponents admit, the possibilities are for divisiveness along broad class, racial, and ethnic lines; the basis of appeal and interaction is broadly ideological; and the potential for militancy and partisanship is higher than one would at first blush have suspected.[23] As Nash puts it, this very intense and broad rhetoric about class and racial genocide will have nothing to do with the merits of the charges or with the motives of the planners.[24] According to our paradigm, such large aggregates of political division tend to be sewn into the nature of constituent policies, whatever the subject or field may be.

These large divisions in constituent politics do not have to be intense, bordering on revolution and repression. For example, the long fight for the eighteen year voting age amendment was large-scale and divided but not particularly intense. Final ratification by the thirty-eighth state legislature surprised many people. However, the divisions are very likely to be national and partisan, in some sense.[25]

Political patterns that have developed around other constituent policies suggest, therefore, that while reeducation and other propaganda approaches to birth control may not be involuntary, they will very probably be divisive on a large scale. Despite the controversy surrounding the Blake and Bumpass-Westoff studies, it is entirely possible, for example, that a future Democratic Party, representing lower income Catholics and blacks, could become the "conservative" voice on population policy, vis-à-vis a "liberal" Republican Party of middle-class suburbia.[26]

This pattern of partisan cleavage could lend a strong sense of excitement and public choice to population issues, and much is to be gained from that. But on the other hand, proponents of population planning could lose everything as a result, if the opposition party happens to win elections on the explicit basis of their opposition to birth control propaganda. This could easily come to be the case if the opposition party goes on to develop supporting doctrines such as defense of the lower classes against the efforts of the upper classes to eliminate them. And it is not at all inconceivable, especially considering the large number of urban and conservative Catholics. A comparable case might be the flurry over state public school requirements to salute the flag in the early 1940s. There the issue was regulatory, but the purely propaganda aspect of the case was not taken lightly by Americanism groups or by civil liberties groups.[27]

All things considered, the constituent approach may be particularly attractive to policy makers because it might produce a kind of national referendum on the whole question of whether the American people want any governmentally sponsored population planning. As a general rule, the fact that the making of constituent policy tends to center in the parties, the judiciary, and in top officialdom may make it a good way to enter into a new venture in intervention whose legitimacy needs fully to be established.

Redistributive Policies and Their
Politics

Examples of important redistributive policies all share one common characteristic: a positive and involuntary manipulation of the structure or environment in which people have families. If we change the Internal Revenue Code so as to tax rather than exempt each child, or all children beyond the second, we alter the privileges and rights for all, without judging the conduct of any. Another policy of the redistributive type would be to set family size as a condition of welfare eligibility. Another would be to support the dependent mother through absolute grants that are not adjusted if her family expands. Another would be to shift tax advantages away from being married and back toward being single.

Redistributive policies are almost self-executing. A marginal change in tax, welfare, or credit rates can have considerable impact regardless of personal idiosyncracies or values of the millions of individuals and families affected by the change. The swiftness of impact may be still greater due to the fact that the lower classes tend to bear the heaviest burden yet are the least capable of organizing for effective political action.

The politics of redistributive policies in general, as outlined in case study after case study, is most often a class-oriented and ideological politics.[28] But its resemblance to constituent politics is rather superficial. Where constituent politics tends to be national and partisan, the cases suggest that a redistributive approach to population planning would more probably be national and executive centered, where the president would find himself in direct interaction with mass publics and with (and against) the spokesman for large, class-oriented groups. The cases also suggest that a large expansion of population controls through redistributive policies might produce upper class cohesion, a phenomenon we have seen little of in our twentieth-century system of federal government, complex economy, and pluralistic interest group structure.[29] But this also might be accompanied by moves in the opposite direction, toward effective organization of the proletariat or spokesmen for the proletariat.[30]

Finally, once a redistributive program is established, the politics tends to center to a larger than average extent in the bureaucracies. But this is not a matter of local bureaucrats and local influentials enjoying a cozy communal relationship, as would tend to be the case for the implementation of the typical distributive policy. In contrast to that, the redistributive approach tends to perpetuate original conflicts throughout the life of the program. Often the bureaucracies in this area end up administering politics as much as money or services. Escalation tends to move up the agency hierarchy toward the department head rather than through local politicians or congressmen.[31]

Thus, although the political process of redistributive policies is more centralized and bureaucratic, dominated by big groups more than by individuals and small groups, it is also more exposed to the public eye, and in that sense is more responsible than distributive approaches to the same problems. Elites may be centralized, but there is greater likelihood of "counter-elites." It is not a partisan politics, in contrast to the constituent arena, but it is focused on alternatives salient to individual voter preference.

However, the risks of redistributive policies are great, especially in the population field. First, redistributive policies increase the social movement potential in the society. Beyond that, redistributive policies increase the movement capacity of the lower economic and racial status groupings; and these groupings are much more unstable and violence-prone when mobilized outside party politics, for mobilization outside party organizations involves charismatic leadership and a grandiose (if not hostile) rhetoric that can destabilize the regime. Concomitantly, the movement potential of the better-off classes is enhanced, and population policy could easily be used by leaders of upper middle-class movements as a mask for repression. Short of that extreme, it is all the more possible to anticipate enough consensus among the upper classes to be able to attach to population control an effective effort to eliminate the very mild redistribution of wealth the revenue system has managed, over a period of forty years, to introduce. That is to say, population policies that work through redistributive techniques amount to a *re*-distribution of wealth. The rich and the poor alike must be punished for having too many children. Suspicions now held about "genocide" among many black and white spokesmen for the poor would begin to appear substantiated if and when the government effort shifted from mildly annoying propaganda to clearly involuntary tax and welfare punishment.

This pattern of severe reaction on a large scale is of course less probable in its fullest realization in the United States than in some already unstable country with runaway population growth. But the tendency does exist in the United States, and other mature countries, as we can see by the Townsend-type and Poujade-type economic movements of the United States and France and the more recent black- and welfare-rights movements in the United States during the 1960s.

Regulatory Approaches to Population–
And Their Politics

Regulatory policies are mainly the ones Professor Nash would reserve for his fourth category, the only category he would clearly label "involuntary."[32] These include: the "first marriage grant" to persons who prove they married after, say, age twenty-five; marketable licenses to have children; permanent sterilization or required abortion after so many births; investigation of all parents and children concerning suspected genetic problems that might make sterilization advisable; requirements of elaborate reporting on the part of all hospitals and doctors in cases of genetic defects, exceeding some set birth limit, or births of illegitimate or welfare children; requirements placed on all doctors to perform prenatal inspection in relation to all genetic and welfare problems and the number of children each mother has had. Such eugenic policies had been anticipated by such liberals as Huxley.[33] After all, it was Holmes, not Hitler, who, in supporting the validity of a state law requiring forceful sterilization of mentally retarded mothers, said, "Three generations of imbeciles are enough."[34]

Other, quite mild, policies include special regulation of businesses whose goods or services have some notable population impact. Drug companies could easily be required to use a significant proportion of their profits on birth control propaganda. Private (as well as public) adoption agencies could be regulated so as to make adoption and foster parentage more attractive to potential mothers and to unmarried females and males. To go to a further but still practicable extreme, health insurance companies could be regulated so as to adjust their maternity services in a way that encourages smaller families.

These types of policies, especially the most effective ones first listed, are least likely to expand significantly in the near future. The reasons for this say a lot about the political pattern of the regulatory approach. Regulatory politics is a great deal more decentralized and unstable than any other type of politics. It is the one arena that tends to be dominated by tightly organized interest groups. In fact, virtually all of the good things pluralists say about pluralism apply with particular accuracy here. This means that one of the significant power patterns will tend to be that new coalitions will form around each regulatory issue. A coalition that is effective in getting one regulatory bill through the legislature can find itself quite ineffective getting the next regulatory bill passed. This is far less true of the political patterns in the other arenas. Interest groups are easier to form and are more effective than social movements or large peak associations like the Chamber of Commerce. But the very specialization of interest groups limits their continuity across issues or their capacity to maintain peaceful coalitions with other groups.

The problem arises insofar as a dynamic interest-group system is too stalemated to arrive at any appropriate policy decisions at all. Dynamic stalemate is not at all a pathological condition for a policy, but reactions to the stalemate can be. When the pressures for some kind of policy decision build to crisis proportion, at least three potentially dangerous reactions are possible. First there is the repression—a decision by governing elites that they can no longer cope with the political situation. This was most clearly the case with the draft in the mid-1960s, where the inability to make it more equitable led first to militant protest and then to the use of the draft powers to remove the agitators.

A second reaction to stalemate is the emergence of a social movement and an eventual redefinition of the policy as a demand for a broad redistribution of power. The best illustration of this will be found after the Civil War when the inability of the states to deal with railroads and other monopolies led to agrarian movements that focused policy demands on a dismantling rather than a reforming of the capitalist system. Schattschneider refers to this political transformation as the expansion and socialization of conflict.[35] Such expansion has policy consequences: It is associated with rather extensive redistributive policies, a far more serious pressure against the very structure of the system than had been implied in the original demands for regulation of the specific evils. In the case of the railroads this meant expansion of policy demands from attacks on price discrimination, rebating, gouging and other monopolistic practices to efforts to eliminate monopolies per se, and to cheapen the dollar and generally to redistribute incomes and power.

The third reaction may be the worst, and it is also the most typical. Rather than have the stalemated regulatory issue transformed into redistributive policies and politics, politicians attempt to buy their way out of stalemate by giving the impression that a policy decision was made. This they do largely by passing statutes in which the real decisions are delegated down the line from Congress and president to lower and lower levels of bureaucracy. When this happens, what started out to be regulatory policy turns out to be distributive, and the politics will change accordingly—toward local irresponsibility. The difference lies, as suggested by the paradigm and earlier discussion, in the degree to which the statute specifies or fails to specify criteria by which conduct is to be guided by clear rules and by sanctions. When effective criteria are involved (and conduct is regulated) the politics of passage and implementation will be dynamic. When policies are not intended to be clear and sanctioned, the politics will tend to come to rest in a reactionary, distributive pattern.[36]

Thus, regulatory policies may be most desirable for all the reasons they are least likely to be adopted. They, among all population control methods, give the strongest appearance of placing the burdens on the rich as well as the poor. They are most likely to provide conditions for defense, retaliation, and reform on the part of those most heavily hit by a particular policy. And they are most likely to enhance the power of Congress over president and bureaucracy: Due to the intensity of specialized interest groups, and the resources of many of them, it is hard for the president to keep things coordinated or committees to keep things contained. Most of the occasions in recent years when the floor of the House and Senate became the center of the political process have been regulatory.[37] That was even more clearly the case during the so-called strong presidency of FDR.[38]

There is no reason to expect otherwise in the population field. The interests involved in these regulatory policies, even the least extreme ones, are far from casual. And if the policies cut various groups and sectors in different ways, the politics is likely to run along those lines, as it has in trade and labor regulation, in the regulatory aspects of public health, communications, and securities.

Policy Impacts as Criteria for Policy Choice

The ultimate moral question, whether the United States should adopt any population control policies at all, is a question for which political science may have no more expertise than physiology, physics, or plumbing. However, if governments in the future are almost certain to adopt many policies to control population growth, it is already beyond the appropriate time to try to work out some criteria to guide them, as well as the people, whose approval will ultimately be sought.

We might begin this consideration with one of the few "categorical imperatives" in the American constitutional system: Civil liberties and personal privacy should be immune from government intervention, except in cases where overwhelmingly clear and compelling justification can be provided. Obviously, this requirement has not led to complete government inaction in abridging civil liberties. Total war has been a sufficient justification. Large-scale natural disasters can provide justification. Rioting and other anarchic or frenzied behavior, when large-scale, may provide justification for abridging some aspect of individual freedom. In fact, the Supreme Court, though generally watchful of the First Amendment and other constitutional immunities, has used such doctrines as "clear and present danger," and the "balance between public need and private rights" to uphold many interventions that, if only by hindsight, were much too repressive.[39]

The original moral question, therefore, turns out in this case to be whether, or under what conditions, the "population problem" is sufficient to justify intervention. No area of human endeavor would seem to be more clearly within the realm of civil liberties and personal privacy than the decision to have children or the decision to risk having children. Moreover, it is difficult to accept Professor Ehrlich's definition of the problem as a "population bomb." If his image came to be accepted, it would justify almost any number and kind of interventions. But there is probably no discrete moment in time when a society reaches such a sudden, irreversible, explosive turn. This is not to deny the seriousness of the problem. The intention here is only to distinguish population growth from clearer cases of sudden disaster, in order to understand the special problem of intervention that can be involved in population policy. Population growth is not yet the "clear and present danger" that justifies government abridgment of civil liberties. In fact, population policy would be a means of heading off the danger. Wherever the danger is anticipatory rather than present, the burden of justification ought to be proportionately greater, if not overwhelming and prohibitive.

To be as pragmatic and permissive as possible, at least two basic political considerations would have to be involved in such a justification—and political is being used here not in its contemporary sense of strategies calculated to influence, but in its classical meaning. The first of these political considerations is constitutional. It is concerned not only with what government has the power to do but with the ensemble of government powers and the gradations and shadings of coercive intervention among them. The second consideration has to do with the impact that these different approaches to government coercion may have on the capacity of people and their institutions to react and to put an end to overly repressive or unsuccessful interventions. Contemporaries would call this dimension of politics "political processes" or "power structures," but an older characterization, "regimes," might be more useful. These two dimensions—constitutional power and regimes, or gradients of legitimate coercion and variations in political processes—can and should be handled simultaneously, for the impact of the one upon the other is not only an empirical question, as this chapter has tried to pursue, but is also a source of criteria for making public choices among alternative routes toward a higher quality of life in America.

Following those guidelines the first policies to be tried would be (1) those for which there is strongest constitutional authority and, simultaneously (2) those whose impact on the American system would be minimal. These two criteria point to policies dealing with problems external to ourselves. No government action has stronger constitutional support than foreign policies, and surely actions controlling foreign phenomena have minimal internal impact. The United States should, therefore, begin a serious population planning program by adopting, and joining with other governments to adopt, policies to "quarantine the aggressor." Concretely this means setting severe limitations on immigration, based upon the population growth rates of exporting countries rather than upon national origin, race, or the other limitations usually put upon immigration.

Although the figures on table 3-3 are not all up to date or as accurate as one would prefer, they do indicate the wide range of rates of natural increase among countries and regions, and they suggest the basis upon which a quarantining policy could actually be formulated. The United States, as well as any other country concerned about world population, could take its own rate of natural increase as the height of the immigration barrier to be raised. Or, it could work out a quota system to discriminate in particular against the countries with the most extreme rates of natural increase. There is far greater justification in this method than in attaching birth control policies as a prerequisite to our foreign economic assistance. The latter constitutes a direct intervention into the internal affairs of the recipient countries, while the former only sets limits on the extent to which the recipient, or any other nation, can displace its population excesses on the rest of the world. Such an approach would be a direct contribution to world population control even as many separate country population growth rates are reaching explosive proportions.

Eventually, however, if not simultaneously, there will be sufficient pressure of reason and public clamor to adopt effective domestic policies to reduce our own rate of natural increase, and the question is what to do first, and why. The

Table 3-3

Rates of Natural Increase: A Selection of Countries, Ranked by Rate of Births over Deaths

Country	Census Year	Births over Deaths Per 1000 Population	Country	Census Year	Births over Deaths Per 1000 Population
Hungary	(1965)	2.45	Canada	(1964)	15.74
Belgium	(1963)	4.57	USSR	(est. 1959)	17.75
Sweden	(1965)	5.77	Israel	(Jewish Pop. 1960)	18.34
Austria	(1964)	6.20	China	(Mainland, est. 1953)	20.59
W. Germany	(1965)	6.21	India	(est. 1961)	21.82
France	(1965)	6.58	Chile	(1962)	22.05
United Kingdom	(1963)	7.14	Puerto Rico	(1965)	23.58
Finland	(1965)	7.25	Thailand	(1960)	26.42
Czechoslovakia	(1964)	7.57	Pakistan	(est. 1961)	26.94
Denmark	(1964)	7.74	Ceylon	(1962)	26.99
Bulgaria	(1964)	8.16	China (Taiwan)	(1965)	27.22
Ireland	(1960-62)	9.60	UAR	(1960)	27.24
Greece	(1965)	9.85	Dominican Rep.	(1960)	27.34
Italy	(1964)	10.09	Singapore	(1962)	28.48
United States	(1965)	10.18	Turkey	(est. 1960)	29.16
Japan	(1963)	10.31	El Salvador	(1950)	33.96
Spain	(1963)	12.42	Honduras	(1963)	34.70
Portugal	(1965)	12.47	Mexico	(1959-61)	34.83
Netherlands	(1963)	12.88	Venezuela	(1963)	36.23

Source: Compiled from Nathan Keyfitz's and Wilhelm Flieger's *World Population* (Chicago: University of Chicago Press, 1968).

principle of judgment has already been established, which is to try policies involving the least coercion before adopting policies involving maximum coercion. The claim to constitutionality will be strongest, and the amount of impact on the political system might also be minimal.

This could mean adoption of distributive policies, because personal choice seems maximal and coercion minimal. However, if the earlier analysis is even fractionally confirmed, arguments against distributive policies, at first or at last, are overwhelming. These policies distribute valuable resources too much on the basis of privilege (which usually means whoever is lucky enough to be near the point of distribution), and the impact on the system tends toward privacy and inflexibility.

This points toward constituent policies, the second category of policy; and this means vigorous education and propaganda in favor of universal family planning. The rates of natural increase in the Western European countries suggest that government programs of family planning and birth control propaganda could in many instances be sufficient. This may be especially promising when we consider that many countries with low rates of natural increase are Catholic countries. An educational approach as a first approximation of population control is all the more desirable if, as earlier analysis has in part shown, education as a constituent policy encourages partisan and electoral activity. After all, this would also mean that population policies after the first serious round might derive more directly from referenda or from issue-oriented electoral campaigns. As frightening as tyranny of the majority may sound, it is nonetheless true that the most legitimate of governmental interventions in private life are those that are based on broad electoral choice.

As effective as education-propaganda programs could be, they are nevertheless high in personal choice; and as a consequence, greater and more immediate effectiveness is likely to be sought. What would be the next step in the escalating war on population growth? And why? Part of the answer lies in our notions of constitutionality and preferred impact on the political system. We can apply these criteria to the next step by arguing that, in matters of public choice, collective or common faults should, wherever possible, be attacked prior to individual variations. For example, a family of ten may ultimately be treated as a violation of a public regulation; however, if a whole community is having an effect on population, that should be dealt with first. In a sense, this is a domestic application of the principle underlying the international quarantine idea, for country birth-death ratios and world population movements are not the only spillover or neighborhood effects to be guarded against.

Because population policy is concerned with "supportable population," it is not a question of absolute numbers or density. It is a matter of definition involving to a great extent the number of people who can be supported at a specified level of comfort in a given place. Therefore, it also involves the level of technology and the efficiency of social organization relative to the density and life patterns in each case.

However, defining the population problem as one of supportability in relation to technology and social organization casts a long shadow across the United States, for there are two kinds of highly probable spillover effects of the great American productive society, one upon world supportable population, one upon the supportable domestic population. Both of these are collective patterns that justify internal controls before seriously attempting to control individual family size.

Just as it is probable that countries with extremely high rates of natural population increase will tend to be aggressors by displacing their population excess on the rest of the world, so it is possible for the most materially productive nations to be aggressors in regard to the ecological effects of their productivity. It must be treated as significant that the United States produces more than 50 percent of the world's goods—a still higher proportion of all war-related goods—because it is also likely that the pollution we displace upon the world is out of proportion to the goods we export. It is far more difficult to measure the displacement of industrial exhaust than it is to measure the exportation of excess population, but it would be completely unjust as a consequence to assume that the pollution and depletion of life supports by the industrial nations is irrelevant to the population problem.

Consequently, enlightened population control policy should step early into the ecology field to regulate the effects of corporate productivity on world supportable population. One important means of limiting the displacement of industrial exhaust is to lay a heavy tax, a regulatory tax, sufficiently burdensome to give corporations the incentive to keep their exhausts close to home. Another would be to require any corporation which exports goods and pollution to set aside a proportionate share of its voting stock for ownership abroad. If we would seek to quarantine excess producers of population, we must also be prepared to quarantine ourselves in regard to our possible aggressions against the world ecosystem. And it is not the sort of thing that can wait for full documentation before action. Just as we have to anticipate the population explosion before we are certain the statistical projections will actually be borne out, so we must anticipate those ecological developments most relevant to supportable population. In both instances, to wait for proof, as though population growth and pollution were like a new medicine for the market, is to be too late to do anything about either.

The second of these spillover effects of collective or community rather than individual behavior has to do with strictly domestic patterns that only affect supportable population inside the United States. To repeat the criterion, before government policy concerns itself with individual family size and individual population-relevant behaviors, it should concern itself with those aspects of community structure and organization that seem to be most relevant to population spillover effects. Let us take suburbanization as an example. Even if it cannot be shown that the suburbs produce too much of the natural increase in actual population, it might be shown that the pattern of suburban sprawl is a variable of tremendous significance in the overall question of supportable population. First of all, suburban sprawl, unless checked by rational planning, can affect the environment far beyond the suburbanite himself. The most obvious but not necessarily the most pressing aspect of this is of course the intimate relation between suburban sprawl and the automobile, which in turn affects the pollution levels and therefore the amount of supportable population—as opposed to the actual size or density of the population. Another, and perhaps still more important, aspect of suburban sprawl is the problem it poses for traditional social control and the provision of basic amenities. Adam Smith opened his classic *Wealth of Nations* with a disquisition on the division of labor, in which he recognized the basic need of concentrated populations for any rational economic endeavor. Jane Jacobs in her fundamental work, *The Death and Life of Great American Cities*, reaffirmed that proposition in her studies of "the need for concentration."[40]

The point of this is that there is a very great difference between density and overcrowding or "too much population." The question is, what *kind* of density? And one can see the problem quite clearly in relation to the American suburb. Suburban sprawl can never support the kind of population that can be supported by a rationally ordered city. As Jacobs observed, when large areas of any community go unoccupied for different parts of the day, as a result of their sparseness or of their functional specialization, these areas become very special problems for provision of services and social controls, as well as special producers of pollution due to the high rates of resource use just to provide basic needs.[41]

Thus, one of the most pressing questions of population policy is how to design urban structures that can take advantage of concentration, rather than how to design escape routes through which to spread smaller populations throughout larger territories. A government that has the rightful power to intervene between persons and progeny certainly has the legitimate power to set limits on community land use. It would be absolutely extraordinary to consider systematic regulations of family size prior to placing systematic regulatory limits on the extent to which communities squander the earth. Forceful land-use planning of this sort will have an immediate effect on supportable population. In contrast, while a governmental assault on family size may ultimately slow rates of growth, this is a very long-run proposition, and the results of such population policies cannot actually be assessed until it could be too late to adopt other strategies.

A further advantage to this approach is that its impact on the political system would be positive. These are regulatory measures and, thus, are likely to encourage the dynamic, organized politics described earlier. Moreover, since these regulations hit whole communities, large corporations, cities, and city and county governments, the burden of the regulations would rest upon those most able to bear it, and the thrust of political action would come from those already organized to provide it. In fact federal regulations of this sort would make the whole American system more dynamic by pitting these organized interests against one another after so many years in which, thanks to distributive policies, they have worked out peaceful alliances with each other.[42]

Finally, if the rate of population explosion is already critical, governments in the United States and around the world are not likely to stop with educational approaches and quarantines on collectivities, even if they are rational enough to try these first. Already we can note plans in the direction of direct controls on individual population behavior, and if Mr. Huxley is correct, the world is already beyond its appropriate time for turning to eugenics as the new religion. Thus it becomes compelling to try to develop a priori criteria by which to guide such efforts, to maximize the impact of governmental programs while minimizing their worst effects. One important criterion that has had a great deal of consensus in the past century, even though often honored in the breach, is to try to place public burdens on those best able to bear them. In operational terms, this means hit the rich before the poor.

Now it is patently obvious that the rich either have fewer children than the poor or can more easily and promptly respond to appeals to reduce their own birth patterns. It is also true that there are fewer rich than poor, and therefore the birth patterns of the rich are less meaningful while at the same time are, by virtue of wealth, more supportable. They do not become charges on the community. However, there are at least two very practical reasons why population policies should begin by distinguishing between rich and poor.

First, the rich have very great bearing on the size of supportable population, even if they are not responsible for the actual population growth profile. That is to say, while the rich are not numerous nor do they have the largest kinds of families, the rich set the conditions of population growth and of supportable population size. Suburban sprawl is primarily influenced by wealthy land developers and implemented by those who can afford to buy and live on suburbanized land. The corporate rich make suburban sprawl almost necessary by moving factories out to areas called industrial parks provided for them by the suburban land speculators. It is also the wealthy and not the poor who profit from converting concentrated city areas into overcrowded areas by allowing the properties to slumify and then by charging the kinds of rentals that make double and triple family apartment occupancy a necessity. As long as there is profit from these patterns, there will be people who will continue to pursue them and as a consequence reduce the actual supportable population in the United States. It is an historic irony that the United States cannot support a population that is small in relation to its continental land mass, despite its marvel of mechanism and despite the astonishing success of its productive apparatus. No governing elite is serious about population control until it is willing to control itself.

A second reason for distinguishing between rich and poor prior to entering into population programs involves the question of legitimacy. The highly sensitive and private business of birth and death requires, as earlier defined, compelling justification prior to intervention. But even with such justification there are strategies that would ultimately be self-defeating. A population strategy aimed primarily at birth rates could easily be taken as a form of suppression, as a preventive form of class and racial genocide. And indeed, if all of population policy were concentrated on birth patterns, exempting from its controls those whose operations and behaviors define the upper limits of supportable birth rates, this would be almost self-evidently a genocidal act of the rich against the poor, the white against the colored races, essentially the West against the East.

Policies that make a pretense of universality are usually hiding coercions that favor the rich over the poor. This amounts to a punitively regressive tax and, as a redistributive measure, would shape the polity in organized classes and movements, much as redistributive politics was earlier described. However, there can be bad as well as good redistributive politics, and the bad case could be one in which the question of legitimacy, rather than the mere shifting of burdens, is involved. Hidden regressiveness would ultimately be found out, especially in something as close to home as population control. Exposure of such deceits could spread and intensify redistributive policies until the very survival of the regime itself came into question. This alone would produce real population control, for violence and other chronic disorders exert strong downward pressure on birth rates. But if that is the kind of birth control we get, we may as well wait for it to happen without bothering with any population control policies at all. If such a public environment as that develops, James Thurber might have been our prophet when he observed, "You might as well fall flat on your face as lean over too far backwards."

If the government of the United States is going to enter this field in any significant way, it therefore should be guided by its own great tradition, and by the errors it has made whenever it has disregarded that tradition. Constitutionalism means government by explicit rules of law, without deceit. Legitimacy means government by consent, and consent requires due attention to the forms of politics that are most likely to produce consent. Constitutionalism, legitimacy, and consent also require redress, and once again that leads to a concern for the political forms best designed to provide dynamic channels for redress. These linkages among American public norms and traditions all point to the reason why political criteria, as defined in this chapter, can and should be the most significant guides to good public policy in any field of endeavor.

Notes

1. David Hume, *A Treatise of Human Nature* (London: J.M. Dent, Everyman Edition, 1952) 2: 239.

2. See also my "Decision Making vs. Policy Making: Toward an Antidote for Technocracy," *Public Administration Review*, May-June, 1970, p. 320.

3. Cf. Herbert Agar, *The Price of Union* (Boston: Houghton Mifflin, 1950), especially chapters 12 and 14.

4. Ibid., and also Richard P. McCormick, "The Imperfect Union," mimeo, 1971.

5. The entire study will be reported in *Arenas of Power—A Reconstruction of American Politics*, now in preparation. Some preliminary results can be found in the PAR article (n. 2) and in "Parallels of Policy and Politics: The Political Theory in American History," a paper delivered to the Organization of American Historians, New Orleans, April 1971; and in "The Four Systems of American Politics: How They Look From the Center," a paper delivered to the Center for the Study of Democratic Institutions, Santa Barbara, July, 1971.

6. This is reported in PAR (n. 2).

7. Paper in progress. See also, Duncan McRae, *Issues and Parties in Legislative Voting* (New York: Harper & Row, 1970), especially chapters 3, 7, and 8.

8. Reported in "The Four Systems of American Politics" (n. 5).

9. Paul Ehrlich, *The Population Bomb* (New York: Ballantine, 1968).

10. A.E. Keir Nash, "Going Beyond John Locke? Influencing American Population Growth," *Milbank Memorial Fund Quarterly* 49, no. 1 (January, 1971): 3-31.

11. One inconsistency would have to be worked out, but it would take further research. Nash's third category includes some "involuntary" measures, yet he explicitly reserves his fourth category for "involuntary controls," implying that the first three are not involuntary. In any case, a concordance between his four degrees of divisiveness and my four types of coerciveness is a promising direction for future policy studies to take. See ibid., p. 16.

12. Ibid., p. 15.

13. See, for example, Arthur Maass, "Congress and Water Resources," *American Political Science Review*, 1950; Maass, *Muddy Waters* (Cambridge: Harvard University Press, 1951); Grant McConnell, *Private Power and American Democracy* (New York: Knopf, 1966), especially Chapter 7; Philip O. Foss, *Politics and Grass* (Seattle: University of Washington Press, 1960); Lewis A. Dexter, "Congress and the Making of Military Policy," in Peabody and Polsby (eds.), *New Perspectives on the House of Representatives* (Chicago: Rand McNally, 1969), chapter 8; and R.H. Dawson, "Congressional Innovation and Intervention in Defense Policy: Legislative Authorization of Weapons Systems," *American Political Science Review*, 1962.

14. See all of the above, especially Maass; also Stephen K. Bailey and Howard D. Samuel, *Congress at Work* (Hamden, Conn.: Archon Books, 1952), especially chapters on patronage (5), porkbarrel (6), and military appropriations (13); and Charles Hardin, *The Politics of Agriculture* (New York: The Free Press, 1952).

15. Woodrow Wilson, *Congressional Government* (New York: Meridian, n.d.) especially pp. 58-81, where he fully describes and indicts "the imperious author-

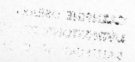

ity of the Standing Committees"; for a general historical review of the policies of that and other periods, see Lowi, "Parallels of Policy and Politics" (n. 5).

16. A systematic reanalysis of a variety of distributive policies in different subject matter areas will be found in "The Four Systems of American Politics" (n. 5).

17. Randall Ripley, "Congress and Clean Air," in F.N. Cleaveland (ed.), *Congress and Urban Problems* (Washington: The Brookings Institution, 1969).

18. Gary Orfield, *The Reconstruction of Southern Education* (New York: John Wiley, 1969).

19. Maass, "Congress and Water Resources" (n. 13).

20. Nash (n. 10).

21. Judith Blake, "Population Policy for Americans: Is the Government Being Misled?", *Science* 164 (May 1969): 524-27.

22. "The 'Perfect Contraceptive' Population," *Science* 169 (September, 1970): 1177-82, quoted with approval in Nash (n. 10), p. 18.

23. See, e.g., Nash (n. 10), p. 18, who, despite considerable optimism regarding this second category of policies, admits the possible emergence of "the militants' charge that such schemes are—given the coincidence of minority racial status and poverty—sugar-coated genocide pills." See also the studies reported and evaluated in *The Wall Street Journal*, 9 August, 1971, p. 1. They report that William A. Darity, head of the Department of Public Health at the University of Massachusetts, found almost half of all black men under thirty in one New England city believed that encouraging birth control "is comparable to trying to eliminate (blacks) from society." This belief about genocide was held despite the fact that about 70 percent of the women the government expects to reach are white—according to the assessment in this article of the provisions of the "Tydings Act," passed in December, 1970.

24. Nash (n. 10), p. 18.

25. Perhaps the best studies in constituent politics are judicial structure and judicial reform, because here we find party dominance despite the sacred position of the judiciary. See, e.g., Wallace Sayre and Herbert Kaufman, *Governing New York City* (New York: Russell Sage, 1960), Chapter 14; see also Richard Harris, "Annals of Politics," *The New Yorker*, December 5, 1970, pp. 60 ff., and 12 December 1970, pp. 53 ff. Historically, constituent policies played the strongest role in the origin and shaping of our party system: see Joseph Charles, *The Origins of the American Party System* (New York: Harper & Row, 1961). For the pattern in organizational and procedural matters in Congress, see L.A. Froman and Randall Ripley, "Conditions for Party Leadership: The Case of the House Democrats," *American Political Science Review*, March, 1965.

26. One might even say that this kind of controversy between Blake and Bumpass-Westoff over how to interpret statistical data is a solid foundation for partisan cleavage among scientists. There will be ample support for honest disagreement.

27. See David R. Manwaring, "The Flag-Salute Case," in C.H. Pritchett and A.F. Westin (eds.) *The Third Branch of Government* (New York: Harcourt, 1963), chapter 1.

28. See, e.g., Theodore Marmor, *The Politics of Medicare* (London: Kegan Paul Ltd., 1970); Frank J. Munger and Richard Fenno, *National Politics in Federal Aid to Education* (Syracuse: Syracuse University Press, 1962); and Bailey and Samuel (n. 14), "The Excess Profits Tax of 1950-51," chapter 12.

29. For example, compare the divisions among the rich and powerful in Raymond Bauer, et al., *American Business and Public Policy* (New York: Atherton, 1963) with cohesiveness of business and their peak groups in something like Marmor (n. 28).

30. Labor is never as cohesive on labor-management regulation or on trade as it is on welfare and tax legislation. Compare Bauer (ibid.) and Alan McAdams, *Power and Politics in Labor Legislation* (New York: Columbia University Press, 1964), on Landrum-Griffin, against Marmor (n. 28) on Medicare-tax issues. For an assessment of how very special these redistributive issues are, even from the viewpoint of the presidency under Roosevelt, see "The Four Systems of American Politics" (n. 5).

31. Because redistributive agencies have longer histories in local government, the best cases will be found there. See, e.g., Lowi, *At the Pleasure of the Mayor* (New York: The Free Press, 1964), chapters 6 and 7; also David Rogers, *110 Livingston Street* (New York: Random House, 1968). At the national level, the best view of this would be through Treasury or Federal Reserve. See, e.g., Stanley Surrey, "The Congress and the Tax Lobbyist," 70 *Harvard Law Review* (1957): 1145 ff.

32. It is unclear why he defines negative tax incentives as involuntary and belonging in his third category, but, in any case, almost all of the examples in his fourth category are regulatory. See (n. 10), p. 16.

33. See, e.g., Julian Huxley, *Man in the Modern World* (New York: Mentor Books, 1948), pp. 28 ff.

34. *Buck* v. *Bell*, 274 U.S. 200 (1927).

35. *The Semisovereign People* (New York: Holt, 1960), chapters 1 and 2.

36. See Lowi, *The End of Liberalism* (New York: W.W. Norton, 1969), passim, where this pattern is called "policy-without-law."

37. See, e.g., the *Congressional Record* on Taft-Hartley or Landrum-Griffin.

38. For example, note J. McGregor Burn's treatment in *Roosevelt, The Lion and the Fox* (New York: Harcourt, 1956): "Quite unwittingly the new President acted as midwife in the rebirth of labor action." (p. 215) "Neither Roosevelt nor Miss Perkins had much to do with this provision (Sec. 7a, NRA). Framed mainly by Congressmen and labor leaders, it was simply part of a bargain under which labor joined the NRA's great "concert of interests." (pp. 215-16). "Roosevelt failed to see the potentialities of an enlarged labor movement. . . . " (p. 216). The Wanger Act "was the most radical legislation passed during the New

Deal . . . [yet Roosevelt] threw his weight behind the measure only at the last moment, when it was due to pass anyway." (p. 219).

39. And the Court is always troubled by each abridgement it has validated. See, e.g., its headaches and reversals in the Flag Salute Cases, in Manwaring (n. 27). Or note its backward and forward motions, its reluctance to issue leading opinions, in the area of criminal justice and the area of the investigatory powers of Congressional committees, in, e.g., Philip Kurland, *The Warren Court and the Constitution* (Chicago: The University of Chicago Press, 1970).

40. Jane Jacobs, *The Death and Life of Great American Cities* (New York: Vintage Books, 1963), especially part 2.

41. See ibid., passim, for her general treatment of the problems inherent in all specialized land use.

42. Cf. Lowi, *The End of Liberalism* (n. 36), and Grant McConnell, *Private Power and American Democracy* (New York: Knopf, 1966), especially chapters 6-10.

4

Some Psycho-political Effects of Population Distribution in a Postsubsistence Era

Alden Lind

In the literature concerning the problems caused by rapid population growth, we are sometimes told that conditions of high density will reduce our quality of life by increasing crime, conflict, tension, and anxiety. If this hypothesis is correct then rapid population growth can create conflict not only because of the reduction of material goods such as food and shelter, but also because of the lack of space between ourselves and our neighbors. This is to say that our "need" for distance between ourselves and others will lead to pathological behavior. In this paper we will attempt to examine this assumption by a critical look at the suburban-urban arrangements in the United States. It is our hope that an understanding of Americans' flight to the suburbs will aid us in understanding the relationships between density and conflict.

America is fast solving a problem which has plagued most societies. It has the capacity now to meet the fundamental physical needs of all its citizens. It remains to develop the norms and techniques of distributive justice with which those who continue to live on the edge of poverty can be brought to a guaranteed subsistence level with respect to food, clothing, shelter, and medical care.

Progress toward solution of the problem of subsistence is not tantamount to the disappearance of problems of interpersonal exchange, however. Entirely new adaptive needs are emerging as human concern shifts from the traditional properties of economic exchange to the more ambiguous and elusive properties of emergent posteconomic exchange relationships. Economic exchange has consisted of highly structured, occasionally ritualized, utilization of well-known units and media of exchange. There has been widespread agreement on the underlying standards of economic value as well as upon the rules of exchange.

As the dominance of the subsistence values, for the exchange of which the economic structure has served so well, has declined, the absence of equivalent exchange mechanisms for postsubsistence values has become noticeable. The resulting "confusion" and ambiguity has provided the stage upon which previously latent consequences of certain American ideological and behavioral inconsistencies have now become manifest. As the dominant influence of the highly structured economic arena has waned, the structural void permitted the emergence of numerous pathological features which had previously been controlled by the relatively unambiguous norms of the marketplace.

Of particular relevance for this chapter, is the wholesale relocation of population which we know as "suburbanization." Many of the consequences of suburbanization are well known. It has created political, institutional, and physical problems and has been blamed for alleged increases in interpersonal and intergroup hostility in urban areas. In its generic form, population distribution and density, it has been touted as a possible "key" to controlling such violence and hostility.

The role of population distribution and density is probably not that direct nor is it likely to be the "key" which, when turned, unlocks the whole of our urban mystery. It is an important variable, as we shall aver, but one whose meaning is rather subtle. In particular, its effects need to be placed in the context of a profound American ideological dilemma.

Fifty years from now, this period will be viewed as one last lunge in pursuit of the most abstract of the many values of American culture; a last desperate effort to capture the mood of unbounded experiential opportunity which has impelled so many to seek this country, to seek the frontier, and to enjoy both spatial and social mobility, directly or vicariously. The traditional concepts of freedom "to" or "from" are inadequate to express this sense of unboundedness, though each is a part of it. More important is the comfortable belief that: "If I wanted to I could, there are no boundaries, and I'm happy conforming to the norms so long as I'm not told that I am bounded."[1] The habit of finding freedom even in a prison cell can be acquired, provided that pressures from the outside are not always reminding one of the walls and the bars. So long as one doesn't become too adventurous, doesn't wander too far from the familiar, doesn't challenge too many barriers, and isn't challenged by too many, one remains relatively free.

The current "unrest" of the young in America is, in a real sense, a very natural manifestation of the American sense of freedom. It is not a working class revolution against the hereditary bearers of wealth and the captains of industry. Rather, it is the children of the moderately well-off—of those who, having braved the anxieties of intergenerational social mobility, have now fled in vast numbers to the protective confines of suburbia—who are reacting to their parents' protection of the status quo. The youths' plea is for "community," for a statusless communion of souls and a profound interpersonal intimacy, for liberation from the protective mores with which their parents have sought to assure their hard-won earnings. It is not surprising that an inconsistency between parental rhetoric and behavior—between their rhetorical insistence on unboundedness and their behavioral isolation—should produce confusion among the young.

The rhetorical emphasis on unboundedness has led the young to search for expressive modes of many types. At the same time they have confronted the garrison state and the modern middle-class suburban nuclear family, both tending to be security and "integrity" oriented, fearing communal and particularistic interaction with others and, consequently, hostile to "boat rocking" and to the suggestion that parental rhetoric and behavior are not entirely consistent. The search for assurance of unboundedness, then, takes the young to interpersonal and communal solutions and to their own inconsistency of communal norms and personal libertarian aspirations. Communities, after all, are not notably free of unambiguous and rigid norms and are frequently more totalitarian in nature than might be a more universalistic society.

Two Approaches to Population Distribution and Conflict

Population and the New Dilemma

The dilemma I have described above is by no means the only form of or basis for political conflict in this nation. Nor is it true that conflict is "bad" in all cases.[2] Yet, certain types of conflict, e.g., racial and intergenerational, have begun to exceed desirable bounds. In addition other forms of social pathology continue to constitute problems, e.g., drugs, crime. The task before us is to trace the sources of the excess hostility and of the pathology.

The dilemma derives from an ideological inconsistency which, in the absence of other critical factors, might not contribute to such excesses. But the move to the suburbs has provided the behavioral opportunities which, in turn, have evoked the clash between expansive freedom-centered ideology and defensive fearful behavioral patterns. It is the interaction of the redistribution of population and the ideological conflict, then, which is critical and which has become such a source of confusion and anxiety.

The assertion of the political relevance of population factors is not new. The Greeks were manifestly concerned with the problem of the ideal size of the polis. Thomas Jefferson felt that population distribution was critical in the determination of the nature of government. Malthus and others viewed population growth as inevitable and with consequences which no conscious political decisions could avoid.

There has been little agreement, however, about the nature of the impact of population change. Jefferson believed that the backbone of democracy was the yeoman farmer who lived and toiled on his plot of land in relative isolation from others of different status. In such a system the distribution of population reinforced the self-sufficiency required by political democracy. Richard Sennett, while intending no honor to Jefferson's position, does it a sort of up-dated justice as follows:

The affluence that has spread to a large part of America in the last twenty-five years has permitted urban, middle-class Americans to create suburban communities for themselves in which the known, the safe, the routine are celebrated and the unknown, the challenging, and the new are excluded. This occurs through the great paradox of our suburban culture: everyone is at once known to his neighbors and yet isolated from them. Each family has its own car, its own yard, its own self-sufficient house; the pain and confusion that occur when people really encounter each other is replaced by "relaxing" sociability where there is no need to deal with another man or woman's inalienable differences from oneself.[3]

The updating, of course, is reflected in the transference of our rural affection to the suburb, the virtues of which begin to sound Jeffersonian. Academic and intellectual celebration of those suburban virtues is, however, relatively scarce. Instead there is much agreement that suburban life is irresponsible, escapist, and ultimately wasteful of resources and human life. Yet people continue to move to the suburbs in their own behavioral approximation of the Jeffersonian ideal.

Rarely does one find arguments which assert the virtues of suburban life. Sennett, for example, argues vociferously for a reversal of the suburban trend by pointing to the increase in hostility and conflict which he attributes to the isolation of the suburbs. He comments: "This hidden fear of the city, this flight into isolation, has concrete political consequences. The search for isolated privacy and the fear of encounter that mold people's feelings about the city are really a scenario for the emotional polarization of society."[4]

Jane Jacobs argues the obvious in her assertion that cities have been the sites of innovation and creativity, of the generation of new lines of activity from the logic of the old.[5] Whether suburbanization is inconsistent with the continuation of such differentiation-inducing effects of urbanization she does not make clear. She does not distinguish urban from suburban, but had she chosen to examine the matter she might have found that the suburban phenomenon had some slight negative impact on the beneficial consequences of urbanization, that the "complicated jumbles of old and new things"[6] which are especially advantageous could not be optimized in relatively isolated patterns of suburban living.

Others have argued that those amenities of life such as symphony orchestras, libraries, and zoos are simply not feasible in sparsely populated areas. Both from the perspective of use and cost efficiency require sufficient population size and density to bring the individual cost-benefit ratio down to an acceptable level.[7]

Whether fear of cities is basically cultural, as Sennett and others contend, or possibly even more fundamentally biological, as Freeman and others have argued, is not the only question.[8] In either case, it is evident that the continued movement from the central city to the suburbs reflects relative assessments of cost and advantage. Such movement also has major political consequences. Those left behind are generally those least well equipped to deal with the problems of urban decay. The city deteriorates as it loses important resources. The consequences to which Sennett refers—the increasing hostility, stereotyping along racial and class lines, and so forth—are also consequences of such population movement patterns.

However, the conflict generated by the fearful escape from the city might well have been generated in even more substantial measure had that escape been impossible. The solution may not lie in simply taking measures to make reurbanization more profitable than continued suburbanization. For all its undesirable consequences suburbanization is a form of sanity maintenance, an effort to relieve some emergent consequences·of postindustrial development by population dispersal from the concentrated central city.

While dispersal succeeds in relieving those pressures, it is in the nature of treatment of symptoms, not a successful effort to grapple with the underlying pressures. The move to the suburbs simply creates new symptoms. The nature of the pathology may change if we move people back into the cities, but it is unlikely that the general level of pathology would diminish.

Density and Conflict

A second school of thought, grounded principally in studies of animal behavior, disputes the Sennett-Jacobs thesis. Proponents of this school contend that population distribution and density have a direct, unmediated, aggravating effect on conflict and hostility. In the animal world, according to ethologists such as Lorenz and Ardrey, crowding and the "spatial imperative" lead directly to an increased probability of confrontation such that intraspecies conflict is increased. Indeed, it is reported that distinctive glandular changes typically associated with changes in levels of aggressiveness occur and persist so long as there is excessive population density.[9]

Calhoun's study of Norway rats, while a contrived laboratory experiment in which density was not allowed to vary freely, nonetheless did establish a high density setting in comparison to the density of the rats' natural habitat. The pathology which developed included numerous deviant modes of behavior, such as bisexuality, maternal neglect, disappearance of normal inhibitions in courting behavior, and high levels of aggression, all of which have been likened to the distinctive behavioral patterns of urban areas. Calhoun coined the phrase "behavioral sink" to refer to the pens in which such pathology developed—pens to which ingress and egress were sufficiently open so that no dominant individual male could establish undisputed suzerainity as was typically the case in the terminal pens of the chain of four, to which there was but one point of access. In those pens, in which the authority structure was quite clear and which, therefore, enjoyed a measure of social stability, the pathology did not develop. The residents of the latter pens were not adverse to the "excitement" of the sink but would retreat to the secure pens in the face of threat.[10]

In addition to evidence based upon animal behavior, we have a limited amount based upon observation of human behavior. In a recent article W.M.S. and Claire Russell identified what they term the "sardine syndrome." They too began with animal studies but subsequently compiled evidence on crime rates and population density in urban areas as well.[11] In Newcastle, for example, the rate of crimes against persons in the most crowded area of the city was five times and the larceny rate four times that in the remaining less densely populated area of the city. A similar pattern was discerned in London. American crime data certainly suggest a higher rate of crime in cities, especially in those parts of the city characterized by high population density.

Anthony Storrs writes as follows:

The population explosion is, of all possible factors, the most likely to cause an explosion of a different variety. The hydrogen bomb is undoubtedly the most effective way of reducing world population: the most fearful expression of hostility yet devised. Who can doubt that, the more of us there are, the more likely we are to be destroyed by the ultimate explosion?

It follows from this argument that to reduce world population, or at least to stem the flood of its increase, is the most important single step which can be taken by mankind to reduce hostile tension. Every other consideration ought to be subsidiary to this, even perhaps our natural impulse to extend charity and medical and financial aid to undeveloped countries. This sounds, and is, a cruel statement. But, wherever hygiene is taught, diet improved, and medical care made available, the result is that within a short space of time there are far more mouths to feed, and the eventual sum of human misery increased by the very methods which were originally designed to relieve it.[12]

Lest one not perceive immediately the mechanism by which increasing population density is transformed so neatly into "hostile tension," Storr's assumptions are similar to those of Derek Freeman who provides the *deus ex machina* as follows:

In broad anthropological perspective then, it may be argued that man's nature and skills and, ultimately, human civilization owe their existence to the kind of predatory adaptation first achieved by the carnivorous Australopithecinae on the grasslands of southern Africa in the lower Pleistocene. At the present stage of progress of human civilization, however, the aggressive disposition which served evolutionary development at various times in the past is perhaps man's most basic and difficult problem.[13]

Man, then, is allegedly hereditarily aggressive. The very survival of the human species depended upon his predatory powers. Increased population density merely increases the probability of hostile, mutually aggressive interaction.

What, then, of the Sennett hypothesis that it is the flight from high density to the low density suburbs rather than the rich interactive urban environment, crowded though it may be, which is to be blamed for the conflict and violence? Sennett relies on the thesis that higher density leads to greater familiarity, hence to lower conflict. But his "joker" is that density alone is not sufficient. The density must simultaneously yield interpenetration of social groups, racial groups, class groups, etc. Then petty differences will subside as men strive to reach superordinate goals.[14]

The ethologists and others who view man as inevitably competitive and conflictual conclude, with Jefferson, that men must be kept separated. Send them to the suburbs, give them their acre and high woven fence and they will be relatively happy and nonhostile. Social distinctions of class, race, etc., are not important. At most, they are limited manifestations of man's occasional efforts to overcome his predatory character by banding into groups; at least, they are temporary self-interest-generated coalitions of beasts which collapse as soon as immediate danger is past and reemerge along new lines as man's predatory nature continues to find new jousts to win. Clearly, however, if this school is correct, we must find an alternative explanation for the revolt of middle-class youth. For having found the serenity of suburbia, they would be expected to have interests in the intensity of communal living as slight as that of their parents and would be predatory in the way of their ancestors. Their primary urge would be to own an acre in a suburb, "just like dear old dad's."

Different Meanings of "Distribution"

It would be somewhat misleading, however, to suggest that population density and distribution play exactly the same role in the two "schools" discussed above. In neither case is it entirely clear that "space" is truly an independent variable. In each it operates to mediate certain human predispositions and human interaction.

Sennett and others of like mind appear to make a series of assumptions affirming the basic civility and benevolence of human nature. While humans desire to avoid the problems of others and tend to withdraw from others in order to avoid the "upsetting" consequences of such problems, the withdrawal is not based upon any aggressive predilection. Thus, with the use of limited amounts of rationality, man can induce social patterns over which individuals are relatively powerless, to maximize the social benefits of interpersonal contact. Just as apartment buildings can be designed to maximize or minimize the probability of unintentional contact of occupants, so could cities and metropolitan areas be planned.

But such arrangements are not intrinsically useful. The Sennett school assumes that these arrangements are useful and desirable because humans are basically friendly when in contact with one another. They learn to cooperate in collective endeavors, and they learn to exchange the fruits of individual effort. To maximize the probability of such collective effort and interpersonal exchange is to reduce the violence and hostility which result from isolation. This is not necessarily to say that no conflict or violence will occur, for, although Sennett does not spell them out, there certainly must be, even in his schema, some values which are sufficiently scarce to induce conflict no matter how high the frequency of interpersonal contact.

Sennett does not, however, see density as a value in itself. It simply operates to maintain a high level of contact and cognizance of common and superordinate goals and interests. Such common and superordinate goals on the whole dominate the few value dimensions in terms of which conflict might be expected.

The ethologist's view is somewhat different, as can be seen in Freeman's work. However, he also suggests that density, or lack of it, is not itself a valued dimension of human existence. It operates to maximize the probability of perceived conflict of interest with respect to other values. Man values food, security, and other "goods" but not necessarily space itself.

This is not always explicit in the ethological literature, however. Ardrey appears to argue that "territory" itself is valued independently of its implications for the other things which men value. Sommer seems to suggest as much in his discussion of cross-cultural variation in spatial preferences.[15] It is not entirely clear that such spatial preferences are necessarily functionally related to other characteristics of the culture, specifically to culturally distinctive patterns of value. On balance, however, it seems reasonable to conclude that the significance of "personal space" is not so much direct as indirect through the effect of spatial variation on the probability of interaction over other generally more important human values, such as food, water, sexual partners, security, and certainty.

The differences between the two schools of thought, then, are not simply reducible to disagreement over the "value" of space but rather to the role of spatial separation in maximizing interaction of fundamentally benevolent and cooperative creatures, on the one hand, or of basically malevolent and conflictual creatures on the other. Benevolence and malevolence are also not individual predispositions but are substantially functions of the value environment in which the individual finds himself.

Political conflict, then, which Storrs rather casually leads us to expect as a direct and inevitable consequence of increasing population density, must be examined in the context of a more complex and inclusive structure of variables—a structure composed largely of value and supply variables which permits us to comprehend how humans incorporate the spatial variable into their "naive" theories of the world.[16]

An Alternative Model of Political Conflict

How, then, do we assess the role of population distribution and density in the determination of political conflict? Let us begin by stating our conclusion in very broad terms: Efforts to impede the flow of population to the suburbs and, more generally, to impede a greater sense of spatial separation, given certain other trends in our society, will result in higher levels of conflict, not lower. Indeed, policy in housing, industrial relocation, transportation, and other areas ought to be deliberately directed toward providing more opportunity for residential and recreational isolation. This conclusion is in direct contradiction to that reached by Sennett.

The next few pages will explore some of the dimensions which intervene between simple density and distribution factors and the level of conflict and hostility. While some of the material may seem esoteric and at times unrelated to the hypothesis, its purpose is to identify and locate in the literature some characteristics of human beings which enable us to understand why, at this point in the development of this nation, population density is operating to stimulate hostility. Simply stated, most value-seeking now occurs in a developmental context in which many Americans are beyond the subsistence concerns of some years ago. This new situation generates anxiety which is maximized by close proximity to other people.

Some Key Values in Interpersonal
Exchange

A first step in seeing why this should be so is the construction of a "model of man" which identifies the major dimensions of political interaction. First, human values—individual preferences—would appear to be ubiquitous properties of any description of human interaction. No theory totally absolves the individual of the role, if not the obligation, of choosing between alternative "future histories" for himself. Some, such as Marxism and theories of Christian predestination, have minimized the expected scope of such volition, but even amongst the votaries of those theories, some have been "more right" with the dialectic or with the "Lord" than others and have therefore exercised relatively more control over the direction of their lives.

Theories of value in psychology, occasionally known as "theories of motivation," are many. Some, notably the instinct theories of the ethologists, but others as well, are likely to view such values as virtual genetic givens. The environment, to be sure, triggers the "innate releasing mechanisms," and behavior directed toward the satisfaction of the related "need" is the consequence.[17] Others of these theories are, at most, combinations of unassailable instincts and learned patterns. Even learning theory assumes some primitive needs to which other patterns of behavior are attached. If Pavlov's dog had not had a prior, and presumably, unlearned "need" for food, he would not have been conditioned to salivate at the bell. Most learning theories, then, are built upon some set of prior and frequently instinct-level needs. Other theories of motivation rely more heavily upon culturally endowed patterns of preference.

Regardless of which theory of motivation is chosen, behavior is seen fundamentally as purposeful and goal-directed, the specific modes of which may be learned or socially "expected." Various theories of motivation have proceeded from that point to posit the existence of lists of more specific values. Guilford, in summarizing work done before 1959, groups his "needs" into five categories: organic, environmental, achievement, self-determination, and social.[18] Maslow, Murray, Lasswell and Kaplan, and many others have their inventories as well. Maslow arranges his in a hierarchy proceeding from the most fundamental, physical needs, through safety, love-affection-affiliation, and self-esteem, to the last, self-actualization. Indeed, according to Maslow, this hierarchy is related by a sort of threshold linkage so that a person is not likely to be concerned with the fulfillment of any particular level of needs until the needs at the previous level are met to some threshold level.[19]

The imputation of hierarchy in needs has important implications, as James C. Davies has pointed out in *Human Nature in Politics*.[20] It permits Davies to argue that there is an inverse relationship between physical deprivation and political activity. Further, and importantly for this presentation, whether the specific listing is precise or not, it sketches the general structure of a system of exchange within a given social system. While any listing of values would supply a basis for exchange, the idea of hierarchy provides us with more information about the probable terms of exchange of such values. It will also permit us to examine temporal change in such terms of exchange for given values among various groups in the population.

Some Significant Values

Of especial importance is one characteristic of human behavior which might well be termed a "value"—the "need to know." Though not especially prominent as a need among those listed by the above mentioned psychologists, perhaps because of uncertainty as to whether it is a biologically given or a derived need, its importance has been discussed in a number of works.[21]

At the most fundamental level, of course, numerous experiments in sensory deprivation and accounts of prison experiences have informed us that the desire to escape such deprivation and seek stimulation is a function of the length of deprivation. The Bexton, Heron, and Scott study in which individuals were to spend twenty-four hours a day for an unlimited number of days in a continually lighted, partly sound-deadened monotonous room with goggles which obscured patterns, with gloves, constant temperature, etc., all designed to minimize the amount of stimulation an individual might receive, showed that human tolerance for such deprivation is quite low. Few made it past the first day. Numerous other experiments in deprivation have shown similar results, with subjects anxious to be relieved of their deprivation in ways which would normally strike them as very boring.[22]

Even under conditions of fulfilled needs at the more basic level of physical survival (including sleep), then, it may be anticipated that humans will continue to seek stimulation. It is not necessarily true that all humans will be equivalent in either the amount or the nature of the stimulation sought. Yet the above findings do suggest the high probability that most humans will be active manipulators of their environment and that such active manipulation may emanate from a less structured and physical-need-bound (in the more traditional sense of that concept) view of human activity than we might have thought.

Even if they seek stimulation, however, is it necessary that they seek information, i.e., nonrandom sets of interrelated beliefs about the operations of the world? Information, in the sense in which it is used here, is not simply the randomly collected paired expectations of events but the formulation of theories concerning areas of purposive activity in which the individual is engaged; theories for which substantiating or falsifying evidence is then sought.

While this activity varies in both its content and structure across individuals, what is of importance is that—whether for instrumental reasons or because it is intrinsically desirable, or both—humans tend to value the reduction of uncertainty and the acquisition of information which reduces ambiguity and makes the acquisition of other values more efficient. The literature on cognitive dissonance is based in large part upon such a premise.[23]

Most theories concerning such cognitive discrepancies view dissonance as a motivating factor much like, if not equivalent to, a "need." The coexistence of beliefs and information which would lead one to mutually incompatible or contradictory behavior, elicits efforts to eliminate incongruence or discrepancies and creates stress and anxiety which the individual attempts to diminish by adopting some appropriate strategy. Behavior may vary from outright denial of discrepant information to the elaboration of more complex theories designed to show that the discrepancy was only illusory.

Additional evidence of the effects of ambiguity and uncertainty—whether a product of insufficient information, information overload and consequent effective randomization of information, or of discrepancies in the available information—can be found in the literature on role theory. Studies by Smith, Steiner and Dodge, and others have led Sarbin and Allen to conclude that "lack of clarity in role expectations does lead to decreased effectiveness and productivity, and . . . these task effects are mediated through psychological effects on the individual which are discernible in such reactions as personal frustration and strain."[24]

Thus, to summarize, persons are inclined to be stimulus seekers, to seek to avoid informationless environments and to seek predictability in their interpersonal relationships. Indeed, the evidence indicates that they hallucinate rather dramatically when deprived of external sensory input to provide focus for the operations of the mind. They also employ various means to reduce uncertainty and the consequent frustration and anxiety about the world which they wish to manipulate. Some minimal level of dissonance-reduction activity, or information-seeking activity, is implied by residual manipulation of, or cognizance of, the world even after more fundamental needs are satisfied.

Where needs such as those for food, sex, clothing, and shelter are left unfulfilled, the focus of the individual's concern and of academic theory building remains on the conditions of fulfillment and the consequences of nonfulfillment of those fundamental needs.[25] The argument we are fashioning seeks to comprehend conflicts in a society which has a large number of individuals whose physical needs have been met but whose behavior is nonetheless perceived to be less than brotherly. It is in such a circumstance that the impact of higher-level needs such as reduction of ambiguity and safety are likely to be felt. We have attempted to indicate that such needs have been identified in the literature. We now turn to consideration of some properties of values which are believed to be related to the ambiguity levels of relationships involving exchange of those values.

Some Important Properties of Values

Human beings tend to value and thus to be motivated to obtain certain outcomes. In general, the more deprived they are of some valued outcome the more they will be motivated to seek it. But how, exactly, do they respond to deprivation? Is it a linear relationship between actual increasing deprivation and its consequential patterns of search behavior? The evidence, while not conclusive, suggests that humans respond in a nonlinear manner to deprivation with activity rates rising in the period preceding the satisfaction of the need and declining immediately thereafter.

Yet humans respond not only to actual changes in the availability of values but also to anticipated changes. Such anticipated changes are based on hypothesized characteristics of values. In particular, estimates of scarcity and divisibility of values are significant. Scarcity, or the expectation of it, is of major importance in Davies' work. He argues that societies are most susceptible to traumatic social change when, having achieved some modicum of ability to satisfy basic needs such as hunger, substantial numbers of the population perceive the imminence of regression to a state of scarcity. Their political activities, once released from the constraints of hunger, are loath to return to the "bottle" from which they emerged.[26]

We occasionally hear of such phenomena as the "psychology of scarcity." Generally the intention in the use of such a concept is to communicate the evocation of a pattern of behavior which includes hoarding and a collapse of norms of sharing, cooperation, and other characteristics of a happy and cooperative community. We hear of it increasingly with respect to our natural resources and, for that matter, our survival. Reports from returning Peace Corps volunteers indicate that societies with subsistence economies are characterized by the absence of cooperative effort, that even community drainage ditches require more collective effort than seems to be easily mobilized. The scarcity of basic necessities presumably accounts for such collective disintegration. While scarcity may occasionally serve as a good indicator of relative value, it is by no means a foolproof estimator. Indeed, the Davies example and others indicate that scarcity may be simply expected, while in other cases valuation may occur independently of either observed or anticipated scarcity.

One would expect scarcity to play an important role in valuation. Valued commodities which are not scarce probably occasion little interpersonal competition or conflict. As most commentators on conflict have noted, conflict is best defined in part as a function of incompatible desired locations in an outcome space, implying some, though not necessarily, zero-sum-level scarcity. And, as argued in the literature on cognitive dissonance, to the extent that either one must compete, or believes he must compete, to obtain a value, one's involvement with it probably leads to increased valuation. Scarcity implies competition which, in turn, implies greater valuation and, no doubt, greater salience.[27]

A social system characterized by scarcity, then, is likely to have relatively little problem with indivisible, collective goods. It is likely to be essentially a barter society with the rules of exchange, if not the relative values of the commodity exchanges, subject to relatively inflexible social norms. Exchange is likely to occur over relatively well defined commodities in a system relatively free of both collective goods and a complex structure of commodity distribution in which the buyer frequently is at a total loss to square the price he pays with the complaints of the producer about the low price he receives.

A second dimension of value, which we have already briefly mentioned, is indivisibility. Some future "sociologist of knowledge" will not be amazed to find that Mancur Olson, Jr.'s exposition of the natural limits on the size of interest groups or Lowi's critique of an interest group ideology should have emerged at this time.[28] As the relative importance of collective goods increases, as is certainly happening in the United States and other developed countries, there is little question that the traditional view of groups will be revised. The view that groups are coalitions of contenders in the political marketplace, with each coalition having a relatively well defined and relatively scarce valued outcome as its target, will need to yield to some reformulation of the processes by which political conflicts are generated.

Man, then, in this formulation (an economic formulation both in its comprehensiveness *and* its view of the structure of the political process) is a multivalued creature pursuing his values through various potential bundles of commodities or outcomes and attempting to minimize costly uncertainty. In the pursuit of those values, he contends with a minimum of two dimensions of those values, namely their scarcity and the extent to which he is compelled by the indivisibility of the value to serve as willing or unwilling fiduciary for others.

The Changing Valuative Context

Unquestionably human nature changes, though it is likely that such changes at the genetic level do not follow smoothly the changing conditions which the human race confronts. Our search for the sources of conflict seems better directed through questions concerning short range and nonhereditary changes.

We have already suggested one fundamental change which confronts the occupants of the developed nations, a shift from the relative clarity of an exchange system in which valued, scarce, and private goods are being exchanged. Not only are indivisible values whose scarcity is difficult to appraise becoming more significant, but also numerous other sources of ambiguity and uncertainty in interpersonal exchange relationships are developing. Two come to mind immediately: The system is increasingly service-oriented as opposed to commodity-oriented, and performance criteria become ever more difficult to apply.[29]

The shift from exchange of scarce, private goods has not, however, been a simple shift to the exchange of abundant, collective goods. Food, clothing, and other commodities which serve to fulfill fundamental physical needs have, indeed, become relatively abundant. Distributive problems remain, to be sure, and their importance will be addressed shortly. However, for a large proportion of this country's population the satisfaction of those elemental needs is not problematic. The increased attention to the uses of leisure time, the four-day work week, and "fringe benefits" attests to that.

But as attention turns from those easily quantified and divisible goods to others, it becomes apparent that the difficulty of assessing scarcity and the terms of exchange increases. Scanning the list of Maslow's value categories, we find, other than purely physical needs, safety, love-affection-belongingness, self-esteem, and self-actualization. A search of the literature reveals no more quantification of any of those than of the notoriously imprecise concept "power." Even safety, which on the surface appears as if it might be measured by such indices as the crime rate, in Maslow's scheme includes order and predictability. Empirically, one would expect to find order and predictability much more probable where the standards of distributive justice and the fidelity of distributive patterns to those standards are more easily assessed than they are with respect to those values in the upper range of the hierarchy. Both scarcity and divisibility, then, are substantially obscured and confused.

Such a change of focus on values accompanies another characteristic of developed nations, the increasing exchange of services rather than commodities. The proportion of the nonagricultural work force listed by the Bureau of Labor Statistics in the "Service and Miscellaneous" category has risen from less than 12 percent to slightly more than 15 percent in seventeen years. Similar rises have occurred in categories such as "Finance, Insurance, and Real Estate" which produce service rather than countable commodities. Not only has attention turned from subsistence-level values to intrinsically less clearly defined values, but even in those sectors of life in which one yet expects to find some clarity in the exchange relationship, such as the economic marketplace, unambiguous evaluation of what one receives for his money is made increasingly difficult.

The increasing ambiguity of performance criteria provides an additional element of ambiguity in the exchange process. Not only is an individual confronted with ambiguity in his role as seeker of values, but increasingly the norms governing his productive behavior are ambiguous. For the expanding number of people providing services, this is relatively easily observed. Both the one who provides and the one who purchases the service are likely to have difficulty fixing the exact terms of trade so that each can unambiguously evaluate the equity of the exchange. Even in those jobs in which easily counted products are being produced, to the extent that automated or assembly line procedures are employed, the exchange of one's labor for pay frequently becomes ambiguous. Where one is coerced by the unyielding rhythm of the assembly line, where one has only limited knowledge of the quality of the finished product, and where one knows that the quality control mechanism frequently adds up deficiencies with limited ability to trace that deficiency to any single person, it appears likely that a worker will lose touch with reality in his bargaining and exchange behavior.[30]

Yet another element of ambiguity is introduced when the population is segmented with respect to salient values. A society divided among those whose fundamental physical needs remain unmet and those who have become members of a subculture in which problems of ambiguity have emerged is apt to have an elevated probability of political and social conflict. Available evidence on cross-cultural exchange processes suggests that neither group will be able to develop confidence that its interpretation of the relationship is accurate. The different sets of premises from which each proceeds in such exchange are likely to decrease the ability of each to predict the behavior of the other and, consequently, to increase uncertainty and defensive behavior.[31]

Conclusion

Our alternative to the Sennett and to the ethological models of conflict stresses the significance of man's symbolic and thinking capability and of constraints on that capability. In the United States in particular, it is becoming more likely that individuals will find old patterns of exchange replaced by new and far more ambiguous exchange practices. The society of "abundance," having substantially fulfilled the physical needs, has now produced a new set of exchange problems which centers on the increasing ambiguity of terms of exchange and norms of distributive justice.

We respond to Sennett's hope that reurbanization will provide "creative" and benign conflict with the caution that the high level of uncertainty and ambiguity in current postsubsistence exchange relationships might produce the opposite effect. It is not simple physical distance which serves to isolate people. Psychic distance, composed of frequent and unpredictable confrontations, is probably more significant.

To the ethologists it is appropriate to respond that the entire pattern of urbanization suggests that under certain conditions high density is preferred to low density. It is not simply crowding which produces violence and hostility, but the collapse of stable patterns which have previously ordered interpersonal relationships.

Some Political Consequences and Opportunities

The nuclear age with its tons of TNT equivalent for every person on the globe combined with increasingly sophisticated delivery systems, has raised levels of both uncertainty and stress. Uncertainty is increasing, however, at other, more obscure, levels of human existence as well. It is perhaps one of the ironies of human evolution that the brain may not be capable of keeping pace with both the information available to it and the increasing need for analyzing and synthesizing that information.[32] As exchange processes become increasingly burdened with obscurity, the mental resources required to account for the new uncertainties increase. Computers and increasing specialization of interest and activities provide limited relief. Psychoanalysis and other forms of therapy such as sensitivity and encounter techniques and the like may well be a natural part of our response. They are specifically directed at eliminating the sources of fixation in interpersonal relations. As the structure of these relationships becomes ever more ambiguous it becomes all the more important that we eliminate atavistic "blinders" in the interest of maximizing predictability. Even the clerics appear to have found that, among those most deeply immersed in the "modern" sector, the problem is no longer so much one of "getting right" with God as it is "getting right with one's fellow man." The substantial pressures in the church for increasing attention to that problem are evident.

Changes in institutional focus, then, and in the relative importance of other institutions constitute one partially political response to the increasing uncertainty in our lives. The emergence of the judicial system as a political institution of vast significance and of the incredible increase in case load, may not be without significance. Where distributive justice becomes unclear one turns to available third-parties for some detached advice on a mutually acceptable solution.

Lowi espouses juridical democracy as a major technique for obtaining reasonable collective decisions. It seems, however, that judicial activity in pursuit of clarity may be appropriate for more than simply combating "interest group liberalism."[33] A substantial reason for it may be the emergence of new sources of ambiguity referred to above.

Institutional modification and change of focus are by no means the only consequences of such dynamics, however. One which has substantial implications for the crisis of legitimacy, with which this nation is frequently said to be presently confronted, is the reemergence of Machiavelli's celebrated "prince" in practice, if not in full regal splendor. A recent volume on Machiavellianism by Christie and Geis, reports that individuals who score high on the dimension of Machiavellianism, those who are both detached and manipulative, tend to perform most successfully in ambiguous relationships. Pertinent to those in university and college communities, they found, for example, that the correlation of Machiavellianism and success in a course, as measured by the instructor's response, tended to be higher in large courses in which the relationship of the instructor and the student was remote and ambiguous. In such circumstances the high-Machiavellian tended to receive higher evaluations than the low-Machiavellian. Such a relationship did not appear in the smaller colleges in which classes were smaller and the relationship between instructor and student was more intense and particularistic. In the former case the relationship was sufficiently uncertain and based upon ambiguous criteria so that the student whose most natural mode of behavior was the manipulative could take advantage of the uncertainty to manipulate the evaluation of the instructor.[34]

While data are difficult to obtain on the temporal changes in Machiavellianism of the nation's political leadership, it is clear that the devices associated with manipulation have become increasingly visible. The "packaging" of a candidate, creating an image for him, the use of public opinion polling and "simulation techniques," all lend themselves to manipulation. Edelman's study of the uses of symbolism in politics, while not longitudinal, does provide us with a framework for viewing the Machiavellian manipulator of mass attitudes.[35] A recent book entitled *The Selling of the President* and virtually all accounts of presidential and other campaigns discuss the role of public relations experts in campaigns.[36] Chester, Hodgson, and Page report their impression that in 1952 "there still seemed to be something vaguely shocking to most Americans about bringing in an advertising agency to sell a Presidential candidate like a hangover cure. . . . By 1968, people had become used to the idea."[37] It seems supportable, then, to assert that the cool, detached, manipulative types are more intimately involved in major decisions about what will "sell" to a candidate's constituents.

Christie and Geis do not force an unwarranted generalization from their findings. They are properly modest in that respect. However, the experimental literature does indicate that as situations become increasingly ambiguous the nature of efficacious political strategies also begins to change. One service which is not provided by these new Machiavellian leaders may be referred to as ideological distillation. Again data are not readily available, but one may find a substantial increase in the number of individuals who perceive no difference between the two major political parties. Politicians are told to find the middle ground and occupy as much of it as they safely can without becoming blatantly inconsistent.[38] This implies ambiguity in the articulation of programs and, consequently, increased ambiguity for the audience. Systematic alternative programs are not presented and, in the absence of sustained, supporting certainty in other sectors of political and social life, the perception of meaningful difference between the parties fades.

The major instruments of policy articulation, the political parties, then, are left essentially sterile. They employ techniques long known in commercial marketing, techniques associated with "product differentiation." They depend upon chance showings of beard stubble or on the choice of bad film footage and on other minor opportunities to gain a tactical advantage. The Machiavellian is not programmatic by nature. He is opportunistic and forever vigilant in his search for sufficient ambiguity or other opportunity to exercise his best manipulative tactics. But Machiavellian strategy provides no opportunity for the cathartic experience of major ideological debate. It does not even provide a meaningful opportunity for the resolution of policy conflicts, which are left to occur in the streets.

Given the increases in uncertainty, one might expect political responses designed to reduce ambiguity in exchange relations, provide more efficient mechanisms for the determination of new standards of distributive justice for less easily quantified values, and to bridge the gap between the subsistence and affluent sectors. Some efforts along these lines have been made by political institutions. Notably the courts appear to be ever more important in this regard, as they become more heavily involved in consumer protection and provision of legal services to those previously unable to find such services. Other efforts have been made through nonpolitical channels. Increasing utilization of psychiatric counseling and the changing role of the clergy are examples.

Some Prospects

This chapter began with a commentary on some current problems of unrest and a question of the relationship of population density and distribution to that unrest. We suggested there that much of the present dissatisfaction might be related to the rather unique interpretation of freedom in the United States, freedom to conform to group norms without the destruction of one's illusions about the unboundedness of one's experiential possibilities. Later we addressed ourselves to the uncertainty which increasingly pervades much of American life as we move from a subsistence-scarcity economy to one in which fundamental needs are satisfied with little difficulty.

We suggest now that as the latter pattern has emerged, the existential problem of freedom has become more salient. In the absence of problems of indivisibility and ambiguity, one's ability to compare situations with respect to constraints and with respect to existential criteria of freedom is relatively enhanced. It seems that this is, in part, the message of Turner and others who have commented on the frontier phenomenon in America.[39] A person reminded of constraints on his behavior could move west where he could view a horizon untainted by fences or other man-made symbols of territoriality. Such decisions were comparatively simple, not only because of the availability of the frontier, but also because one could have some subjective confidence.

Both exchange and freedom, then, are more problematic in societies in which the fundamental needs have been adequately fulfilled, because of the increased difficulty of attaining explicit and meaningful terms of exchange: Part of the early American solution to dissatisfaction with exchange and freedom was to seek open territory, to move west where one could establish more favorable conditions. As the problems of exchange and freedom intensified, a new exodus occurred, the flight of those of relative prosperity to the suburbs where they took refuge from the confusion behind hedges and fences and insisted that this was freedom. This exodus was probably not so much a result of conflict bred by excessive density in the city as it was by the psychic torment of uncertainty. The suburbanites were attempting to reduce stress by isolating themselves. The escape may not have been so much from crime and other urban phenomena of that type as it was from the constant reminder that one wasn't certain that he was not being taken advantage of, that his freedoms were not being abridged. However, escape to the suburbs was not simply an effort to isolate oneself. With adequate space and a proprietary right in one's property, one could manage both to sustain one's acquired perquisites and expand one's sense of control by participating in the "do-it-yourself" craze or by purchasing a boat and escaping to the open spaces of the nearest lake where one was the "master" of his ship. It would appear that the illusory aspect of escape as well as its inconsistency with the professed norms of total autonomy have begun to become visible to the children of the suburbanites.

What then of the conflict between those who argue that cities are "behavioral sinks" and ought to be broken up, that we ought to return to the Jeffersonian ideal or as near to it as possible, and those who argue that the city and high population density are the only way in which to break down the rural and suburban isolation which breed hostility and conflict? We have tried throughout this chapter to argue that density of population is not the essence of the present problem in human relations in this country. Man's ability to think, to symbolize, to create, to solve basic problems of survival and, subsequently, to focus on more abstract problems of human interrelationships has created a condition in which his information acquisition and utilization capabilities have been outrun by the demand for certainty and the supply of information. Various techniques have been employed in the effort to redress this deficiency. Psychological, technical, religious, and spatial solutions have been tried. Thus far, none has obviously been successful.

Suggestions by Sennett and by certain architects such as Soleri that we may solve our problems of excessive hostility and conflict by building or rebuilding our cities and encouraging people to move to them appear somewhat futile. Increasing the density will immediately intensify the problems which so many have attempted to escape by moving to the suburbs and which so many others cannot afford to escape in the same manner. What little increment of control over one's life a move to the suburbs provides will not be offset under present conditions by moving back to the city. Sennett and others who argue that increasing density increases useful confrontation appear to overlook the following: The major confrontations occur among groups *within* the city. These groups enjoy relatively high frequency of contact, but their abilities to reconcile differences are sapped by social and cultural segmentation (those who have solved the basic subsistence problems and those who haven't), by uncertainty and confusion, by the emergence of Machiavellian leadership, and by the emergence of critical problems requiring collective decisions about relatively indivisible problems.

A more theoretically sound, though not necessarily more "practical," proposal would seem to be one which optimally mixes the following ingredients: (1) reasonable dispersion of population so as to effect some semblance of subjective personal efficacy; (2) utilization of public policy to encourage "mixed" low density residential areas, schools, and places of employment; (3) self-conscious and deliberate modification of the national myth-system in view of the emergent difficulty in assessing one's identity, worth, and freedom in terms of quantifiable commodities such as goods and bank-accounts and in view of the incredible waste through product differentiation as we attempt to sustain the myth-system; (4) improvements in avenues of recourse for consumers of "anonymous products" and services which are difficult if not impossible to evaluate; (5) improvement of information systems available to the public and increased training of young people and adults in their utilization; (6) simplification of collective decision processes by replacement of the incredible array of political institutions which we now have with a more centralized structure giving special attention to facilities for mediation, negotiation, counseling, (as Lowi so ardently wishes, "interest group liberalism," in the sense of government as "adding machine," must go); (7) equalization of distribution of subsistence commodities, including health care, so as to eliminate the increment of hostility due to maldistribution of such commodities.

No doubt other measures will be called for. But unless they take account of the complex interrelations of psychological, spatial, and economic-political exchange factors they will be at best accidentally helpful. Manipulating population density and distribution patterns by themselves will not prove helpful. High population density, i.e., urbanization, appears to be a necessary component of development, but as we have argued, its effects vary as development occurs. What will be the consequences of population growth and the consequent increase in density cannot be predicted accurately without consideration of the possibility of change in the other areas we have discussed.

Notes

1. This notion is particularly apparent in the responses of Robert Lane's respondents to questions about freedom. They are reported in Lane's *Political Ideology* (New York: Free Press, 1962).

2. The functions of social conflict are discussed in many places, perhaps most notably in Louis Coser, *The Functions of Social Conflict* (Glencoe, Illinois: Free Press, 1956) and in Georg Simmel, *Conflict* (Glencoe, Illinois: Free Press, 1953). Kenneth Boulding has a nice discussion of conflict in chapter 15 of his *Conflict and Defense* (New York: Harper and Row, 1962) which presents a view acceptable to me concerning the scope and nature of the problem of conflict.

3. These comments appear in two articles which Richard Sennett contributed to the guest column series in the *New York Times* of October 19 and 20, 1970. The Jeffersonian versions can be obtained in various locations. One abbreviated source is John Dewey (ed.), *The Living Thoughts of Thomas Jefferson* (New York: David McKay), 1940.

4. Sennett, ibid.

5. Jane Jacobs, *The Economy of Cities* (New York: Random House, 1969).

6. Ibid., p. 250.

7. See, for example, Otis Dudley Duncan, "Optimum size of cities," in J. Spengler and O.D. Duncan, *Demographic Analysis* (Glencoe, Illinois: Free Press, 1956).

8. Derek Freeman, "Human Aggression in Anthropological Perspective," in J.D. Carthy and F.J. Ebling, (eds.), *The Natural History of Aggression* (New York: Academic Press, 1964).

9. See among others: Konard Lorenz, *On Aggression* (New York: Harcourt-Brace and World, 1966); Robert Ardrey, *The Territorial Imperative* (New York: Dell Publishers, 1966); on the physiological correlates of aggressive behavior, two volumes provide substantial data: Carthy and Ebling (n. 8) and S. Garattini and E.B. Sigg, (eds.), *Aggressive Behavior* (New York: Wiley, 1969).

10. J.B. Calhoun, "Population Density and Social Pathology," in David Heer (ed.), *Readings on Population* (Englewood Cliffs, N.J.: Prentice-Hall, 1968).

11. Their report was summarized in an article in the *New York Times*, 16 August, 1970.

12. Anthony Storrs, *Human Aggression* (New York: Atheneum, 1968), p. 120.

13. Freeman (n. 8), p. 116.

14. These ideas would be in line with those of Muzafer Sherif in *Group Conflict and Cooperation* (London: Routledge and Kegan Paul, 1966).

15. Robert Sommer, *Personal Space* (Englewood Cliffs, N.J.: Prentice-Hall, 1969). Also see Edward T. Hall, *The Hidden Dimension* (Garden City, N.Y.: Doubleday, 1966).

16. The general view of the nature of interpersonal relations used here is

contained in Fritz Heider, *The Psychology of Interpersonal Relations* (New York: Wiley, 1958). The concept "naive theory" is developed there.

17. An excellent coverage of this material is provided by C.N. Cofer and M.H. Appley, *Motivation: Theory and Research* (New York: Wiley, 1967).

18. J.P. Guilford, *Personality* (New York: McGraw-Hill, 1959).

19. The other works mentioned in that paragraph are: A.H. Maslow, *Motivation and Personality* (New York: Harper, 1954); H.A. Murray, *Explorations in Personality* (New York: Oxford University Press, 1938); H. Lasswell and A. Kaplan, *Power and Society* (New Haven: Yale, 1950).

20. New York: Wiley, 1963.

21. This "need to know" is presented differently in at least two works. Leon Festinger in two articles, "A Theory of Social Comparison Processes," *Human Relations* 7 (1954) and "Motivations Leading to Social Behavior," in M.R. Jones (ed.), *Nebraska Symposium on Motivation* (Lincoln: University of Nebraska Press, 1954), argues essentially that the need is innate. J. Dollard and M. Miller, *Personality and Psycho-therapy: An Analysis in Terms of Learning, Thinking, and Culture* (New York: McGraw-Hill, 1950), appear to indicate that the need to know is learned through differential reinforcement of incorrect and correct reporting of the world. Both agree, however, that such a need does operate in human behavior.

22. See particularly W.H. Bexton, W. Heron and T.H. Scott, "Effects of Decreased Variation in the Sensory Environment," *Canadian Journal of Psychology* (1954).

23. Two major works on cognitive dissonance in which this view of dissonance is quite clear are: Leon Festinger, *A Theory of Cognitive Dissonance* (Stanford: Stanford University Press, 1957) and Jack Brehm and Arthur Cohen, *Explorations in Cognitive Dissonance* (New York: Wiley, 1962).

24. Theodore Sarbin and Vernon Allen, "Role Theory," in Gardner Lindzey and Elliot Aronson (eds.), *The Handbook of Social Psychology*, 2nd ed. (Reading, Massachusetts: Addison-Wesley, 1968).

25. Davies (n. 20) and Ted Robert Gurr, *Why Men Rebel* (Princeton: Princeton University Press, 1970).

26. Davies (n. 20).

27. There seems to be little disagreement on this general proposition. See G.W. Allport and B.M. Kramer, "Some Roots of Prejudice," *Journal of Psychology* 22 (1946); G. Lindzey and S. Rogolsky, "Prejudice and Identification of Minority Group Membership," *Journal of Abnormal and Social Psychology* 45 (1950); L. Postman, J. Bruner, and E. McGinnies, "Personal Values as Selective Factors in Perception," *Journal of Abnormal and Social Psychology* 43 (1948).

28. Mancur Olson, Jr., *The Logic of Collective Action: Public Goods and the Theory of Groups* (Cambridge: Harvard University Press, 1965) and Theodore Lowi, *The End of Liberalism* (New York: Norton, 1969).

29. That this shift to service orientation has major consequences has been

argued by Daniel Bell, "Notes on the Post-Industrial Society," *The Public Interest*, Winter and Spring issues, 1967. While this part of my argument parallels some of Bell's argument, the critical role of emergent cognitive problems in a developed society are not discussed by Bell.

30. The relationship between political attitudes and one's occupational role is nicely shown in Lewis Lipsitz, "Work Life and Political Attitudes: A Study of Manual Workers," *American Political Science Review* 58 (December 1964).

31. I use the term "likely" here, for we know little about the effects of cognitive convergence on intergroup or even interpersonal conflict. I intend to address myself more fully to this matter in a subsequent paper. Literature in such diverse areas as international relations, community politics, and on role reversal studies indicates our frequent presumption that building shared "understandings" of a situation will lead to lower levels of conflict. Witness Ralph Gerard, "To Prevent Another World War: Truth Detection," *Journal of Conflict Resolution* 5 (1961), and Anatol Rapoport, *Fights, Games, and Debates* (Ann Arbor: University of Michigan Press, 1960). Both at times employ the argument that agreement about the nature of a situation is likely to lead to reduction of hostility. While this is undoubtedly true in some situations, it remains an open question how we identify those in which it is and those in which it isn't.

32. James C. Davies, in correspondence, has suggested that I may "underestimate the brain's ability," especially given that ordinary people are probably now far more able to "absorb and appraise" information than they were, say, in the sixteenth and eighteenth centuries. He raises a critical point which, unfortunately, I cannot consider in any detail here. He cites decrease in violence as an indicator of greater tolerance of ambiguity and, presumably, of the utilization of more of the available information, yet that reduction might be a product of other operative factors possibly including more skillful manipulation by elites. We do know that there are physiological limits on the ability of the brain, however. Professor Davies and I differ slightly in our estimate of how near "saturation" we are at the moment. But, perhaps more importantly, the nature of available information may well be much more inconsistent and ambiguous now than previously. Thus, both convergence on saturation and overwhelming demand for additional and frequently costly or unobtainable information, may contribute to the effective level of ambiguity at which the person operates.

33. Lowi (n. 28), pp. 297 ff. In Lowi's argument the courts enforce statutory clarity, and administrative rule making then is used to regularize the agency-client relationship.

34. Richard Christie and Florence Geis, *Studies in Machiavellianism* (New York: Academic Press, 1970).

35. Murray Edelman, *The Symbolic Uses of Politics* (Urbana, Illinois: University of Illinois Press, 1970).

36. Joseph McGinnis, *The Selling of the President* (New York: Pocketbooks, 1969).

37. Lewis Chester, Godfrey Hodgson, and Bruce Page, *An American Melo-drama* (New York: Viking Press, 1969), p. 712.

38. Richard Scammon and Ben Wattenberg press this point in their volume, *The Real Majority* (New York: Coward-McCann, 1970).

39. Frederick Jackson Turner, *The Frontier in American History* (New York: Holt, Rinehart, Winston, 1920).

5

The Effective Population in International Politics

A.F.K. Organski, Bruce Bueno de Mesquita, and Alan Lamborn

This chapter will outline some of the major connections that can be established between population trends and national power and security. Admittedly some of the links are tenuous due to the necessity of tracing them through a maze of intermediate variables. Certainly a full picture of the many connections would show them to be exceedingly complex and only imperfectly understood. Nevertheless, it seems important to investigate, even in an initial fashion, some of the ways in which demographic shifts affect the power and security of the nation, for the results of such an investigation are instructive in giving policy makers some perspective about what can be changed and what cannot.

It should be made clear at the outset that when national power and security are referred to here, the reference is not primarily to military preparedness. By *power* is meant the ability of the nation to manipulate its international environment, particularly its ability to influence the behavior of other nations and to withstand unwelcome influence on their part. By *security* is meant the safety of the nation from armed attack, internal subversion, or damage to its vital international interests. Military preparedness is but one of many factors affecting a nation's power and security and does not, in itself, guarantee any predictable result.

Consider, for example, the association between military preparedness and the long-run power and security of the major combatants in World War II. The ultimate in military preparations did not save Germany and Japan from defeat at the hands of the woefully unprepared United States and Britain. The French, according to some calculations, were more prepared than the Russians, but France fell and the Soviet Union did not. The Italians were terribly unprepared militarily, and were disastrously defeated. Nor has military preparedness provided either the Egyptians or the South Vietnamese with security. The picture at best is muddled; a causal link between preparedness and power and security is still to be made.

Power, it is generally agreed, is that facet of every human relationship that enables the parties to the relationship to influence or control each other's behavior. Joint behavior, essential in any relationship, would not be possible but for the mutual influence that the parties exercise over one another. Among nations, this influence is exercised through a wide range of means of which military force

This is a slightly revised version of a paper submitted to the Commission on Population Growth and the American Future. The authors wish to acknowledge their indebtedness to Mr. Jack Kugler who did much of the accumulation and analysis of the data on which this chapter is based.

is only one. The methods of exercising power can be broadly categorized as: persuasion, reward, punishment, and force, and in the daily course of international relations the overwhelming number of pressures applied by nations to one another are exercised by methods other than military force. Similarly, the determinants of national power include many variables other than the size of a nation's military forces and the degree of their preparedness.

When it comes to considering the determinants of national power, there is an additional difficulty which must be faced. The conception of national power is notoriously defective in lacking an objective, independent measurement. Used as a dependent variable, it creates immense difficulties, for there is no way of measuring it independently from its determinants. Thus we customarily assess a nation's power by its population size, its economic might, or even the size of its military forces, all of which, of course, are partial determinants of power but not the power, itself. To measure directly the "quantity" of influence that one nation in a complex system exercises over all the others is theoretically possible, but has never been done. Direct indications of the relative power of nations are given when one defeats another in a war (but only if they fight without allies, and even then other factors may tip the balance. Surely no one would claim that the United States is less powerful than North Vietnam despite the fact that the United States cannot seem to win the war between them). War, however, is not the usual state of affairs among nations, and we more generally estimate their relative power by falling back upon an impressionistic weighting of the probabilities that a nation will get its way in a conflict of interest with others. In consequence, the relative importance of the various determinants of national power is customarily judged by their correlation with this impressionistic power ranking. The methodological deficiencies are clear but seem unavoidable at this stage in the study of international relations. It is certain that the deficiencies are not removed by failing to mention them.

Caveats aside, the three variables generally considered the most important of many determinants of national power are: population size, level of economic productivity, and level of political mobilization. Our concern here is primarily with the demographic determinants of power and with their interrelationship with economic productivity and political mobilization.

The rationale for considering population size a major determinant of national power is fairly clear. After all, it is people who fight and work and consume and carry within themselves the national culture and ideology, and it is these activities that are the sources of the capacity of one nation to influence the behavior of other nations. At times, however, people may do none of these things, and in such cases they add nothing to a nation's power. These divergent possibilities are summed up in the following passage:

Population is, indeed, a nation's greatest resource, though like other resources it may be squandered or misused. What greater asset can a nation have than a multitude of able-bodied citizens, ready to stoke its furnaces, work its mines, run its machinery, harvest its crops, build its cities, raise its children, produce its art, and provide the vast array of goods and services that make a nation prosperous and content? On the other hand, what greater liability can a nation have than a mass of surplus people, living in hunger and poverty, scratching at tiny plots of land whose produce will not feed them all, swarming into cities where there are no more jobs, living in huts or dying in the street, sitting in apathy or smouldering with discontent, and ever begetting more children to share their misery? The relationship between numbers and wealth and power is not simple, but surely it is significant.[1]

Total population size sets limits to a nation's power, but they are broad limits, and within them considerable variation is possible. The variations are shaped by the way demographic, economic, and political variables are intertwined, and it is these variations that influence the relative power of nations.

The Effective Population

For purposes of national power, a nation is no larger than the portion of its population that makes a contribution to the furthering of national goals. We call these people "the effective population."[2] If effective populations rather than total populations are considered, some startling results are obtained. Consider, for example, a list of the most populous nations in the world: those with total populations above 50 million. More than two-thirds of the people on earth live in these thirteen nations. Eight of them are giants, two of them what might be called super-giants. Yet if only the effective population is counted (by procedures to be explained later), some of these nations shrivel up unbelievably. China, for example, shrinks to less than one-tenth her total size, while Indonesia has an effective population smaller than the number of people living in greater New York City (see tables 5-1 and 5-2).

The tremendous gap between total population size and effective population size becomes significant when we consider that it is changes in the effective population that are most likely to bring future increments of power. Total population size sets limits to how large the effective population can become, but the nation with a low percentage of its population making an effective contribution contains an immense reservoir of untapped power compared to the nation like the United States that is already using its population relatively effectively.

Of course, one must consider not only the size of the effective population but also the level of their skills and the ability of the political and economic system to aggregate individual contributions into a common pool of national capabilities to be used in furthering national goals. These factors in turn are interrelated in intricate and subtle ways. For example, the level of individual skills is very much a function of the system, which not only facilitates or hinders the training of individuals but also affects their willingness and their commitment to national goals.

In summary, to assess the contribution that a nation's population makes to its power, we must ask four different questions:

1. How many people does a nation have?
2. How many of them now make, and in the future could make, a contribution to the achievement of national goals?
3. How motivated, skilled, and productive are they?
4. And how successfully can their individual contributions be pooled in the joint pursuit of common national goals?

Let us address ourselves to each of these questions in turn.

Size of Total Population

Few attributes of nations vary more than population size. Political entities vary in size from China with its 740 million people down to Pitcairn Island with a population of 75.[3] The "typical" nation has a population under 10 million and does not possess much international power. The vast majority of political units (168 out of 219) fall into this category, which includes such independent nations as Ghana and Haiti, Israel and Jordan, Cambodia, Albania and Ireland, and all of the world's remaining colonial territories.

The major world powers all have populations of at least 50 million. A population of this size appears to be at least a prerequisite of great power status, though not a guarantee (see table 5-1). The two great superpowers (and their most troublesome rivals: China and Japan) have populations of over 100 million.

Total population size alone provides at least a partial explanation of the diminishing importance of the West European powers that dominated the world in the nineteenth century. They simply do not possess the demographic resources to compete with nations four times their size once these nations become economically developed and politically mobilized.

On the basis of their size, the United States and the Soviet Union appear assured of continued leadership for some time to come but face clear future threats from China (increasingly recognized), India (generally overlooked), and a United Europe if true political unity is ever achieved.[a]

Size of Effective Population

Total population size is interesting in that it sets limits to the size of the effective population and provides an indication of future possibilities, but for an

---

[a]The combined population of the Common Market nations plus Britain (mid-year, 1969) is 243 million, a population larger than that of either the United States or the USSR.

Table 5-1
Nations with Largest Total Populations

Nation	Population in Millions[a]
China	740
India	537
USSR	241
United States	203
Indonesia[b]	117
Pakistan	112
Japan	102
Brazil	91
Nigeria	65
West Germany[c]	61
United Kingdom	56
Italy	53
France	50

[a]Midyear, 1969. United Nations, *Statistical Yearbook, 1970* (New York: United Nations, 1971), table 18.
[b]Including West Irian.
[c]Including West Berlin.

understanding of the relative power of nations at the present time and in the near future, the size of the effective population is more significant.

The majority of the people in any nation do not make any significant contribution to the nation's power, either through economic production, political participation, the payment of taxes, or military service. In the United States, for example, 58 million Americans are under the age of 15. They will make no contribution to the achievement of national goals until they work, fight, or vote, activities which some of them will not pursue until they are into their twenties. In the meantime, their activities and their welfare are of the greatest national interest. Indeed, matters concerning them provide the focus of many of the nation's most controversial political issues: racial integration in the schools, the draft, drug addiction, crime. It is legitimate to view this large group as valuable in themselves, and it is reasonable to regard the immense expenditures of resources and energy on their behalf as investments in the nation's future, but for the duration of their juvenile dependency they consume but do not produce, they question but do not make decisions, they disrupt but do not unify. At best, they prepare. In short, they are not part of the nation's effective population. Neither are most of the 20 million Americans aged 65 and over, though some continue to be economically and politically active.

Even within the 15-65 age group there are many who make no effective contribution to the achievement of national goals: the physically ill, the mentally deranged, the criminal, the disaffected, or simply the unemployed. In terms of political participation it is worth noting that out of 118 million Americans of voting age, only 73 million actually voted in the last presidential election.[4] The number who join political parties or campaign actively is much smaller.

When it comes to taxes, virtually all adult Americans contribute something to the federal government through income taxes and excise taxes, but the contribution is often small. In 1967, only 34 million Americans paid federal income taxes of more than $500.[5]

The contribution made through economic production is perhaps the hardest to assess. Most adults "work"; that is, they produce some economic goods or service. The subsistence farmer who grows his own vegetables produces economic goods, but they are immediately consumed within his own family. We can make a distinction between workers who take care of themselves and their dependents and those who are involved in economic networks that enable them to make economic contributions to others outside the household and beyond the village, contributions that can be used to achieve national goals. The peasant in a subsistence economy does make a contribution to others. We would classify him not as a dependent but as a "noneffective." And for our purposes we would probably be justified in classifying most housewives in the same manner. On the other hand, the farmer in commercial agriculture and the woman in paid employment are both part of the effective population.

We are dealing here with a continuum of contribution. The contribution to national power is obvious in the case of those who help produce military goods or those who produce commodities that are exchanged in international trade. It is clear for those who produce raw materials or foodstuffs for the rest of the nation. It is visible for most of those who produce the goods and services that make up the gross national product, and it is perceptible for the housewife who provides economic services for her husband who in turn provides economic services for the rest of us. It has just about vanished for the man who provides only for himself, though he may pay taxes, or for the dependent student, though he may suddenly be drafted.

For purposes of international comparison we must arbitrarily decide who is in the effective population and who is not, but, in reality, the problem is complicated not only because the level of contribution varies but also because some people contribute in one area and some in another. In some cases the contribution is intermittent and in others it is continuous. Moreover, specific individuals drop in and out of the effective population. Sick people get well again, peasants are drafted and then return to the fields, students become politically active, workers become unemployed.

The indicator used here for the effective population, although crude and thus obscuring these fine distinctions, is the number of employed nonagricultural workers. It has the merit of excluding the dependent groups: children, the aged, the infirm, the unemployed. For the developing nations, it also separates out in a rough way the modern sector from the traditional sector of the economy. Also, and this is essential, economic data of this nature are available for a relatively large number of countries.

There are also marked liabilities, however, in using such a measure of effective population. In the first place it discriminates only economic effectiveness and omits other information in which we may be very much interested, such as the number of politically active people and how well they are organized. When we measure the effective population of China, for example, it totals the economically effective but gives no clue as to the contributions to power made through the political system. This is a grievous defect.

Even in economic terms, the measure is inexact, for it excludes people who, on strong theoretical grounds, should be counted as effective. It is clearly incorrect to exclude from the ranks of the effective population people who work in agriculture in developed countries. In the most highly developed countries agricultural workers not only make a contribution to the national economy but, indeed, are among the most efficient workers in the nation. In the United States, for example, gains in productivity in agriculture have been so high that a tiny fraction of the working population has become capable not only of taking care of the needs of the nation but of producing surpluses for export to millions of nonnationals as well. Throughout the developed nations, a major feature of social and economic modernity has been the small fraction of the labor force who work the land. The distortion resulting from excluding modern farmers from the effective population is therefore minimized by the fact that the numbers involved are relatively small, but it is still a distortion.

The indicator used (number of employed nonagricultural workers) also excludes the military, for in most cases the figures available on occupational breakdowns are for the civilian labor force. This, too, is a group that certainly ought to be included as contributors to the realization of national goals. Not only do military forces contribute to national defense, but in countries such as China they also provide a considerable amount of labor for such tasks as road-building and construction. The idea of an effective population is valid, but the indicator is faulty.

In spite of its shortcomings, the yardstick we have chosen gives some striking results when used for international comparison of effective populations (see table 5-2). China still heads the list, but like the other nondeveloped nations she has shrunk to a fraction of her total size, so small a fraction that her effective population is scarcely larger than that of the United States despite the much larger total population base from which she starts. The United States, using her population more effectively, has a larger effective population than the USSR, although her total population is smaller. The United Kingdom, though having a high percentage of effective population, is nevertheless seventh in world ranking, for her total population is simply not large enough to provide her with sufficient base.

Table 5-2
Nations with Largest Effective Populations

Nation	Effective Population (number of employed nonagricultural workers in millions)[a]	Percentage of Total Population in Effective Population
China[b]	62.1	10%
United States	60.5	33%
USSR	58.0	27%
India[c]	38.0	9%
Japan	31.1	33%
West Germany	22.8	42%
United Kingdom	22.2	42%
France	14.7	32%
Italy	14.0	28%
Indonesia[c]	8.6	9%

[a]1961. Except for China, India, and Indonesia, all figures are computed from International Labour Office, *Year Book of Labour Statistics, 1970* (Geneva: International Labour Office, 1970), table 3.

[b]1959. Data computed from Chi-Ming Hou, "Manpower, Employment and Unemployment," in Alexander Eckstein et al. (ed.), *Economic Trends in Communist China* (Chicago: Aldine, 1958).

[c]Figures include unemployed, so are slightly inflated and not strictly comparable. Computed from United Nations, *Demographic Yearbook, 1964* (New York: United Nations, 1965), table 9.

It is instructive to consider the percentage of the total population that is included in the effective population for the major nations, for it shows how heavy a load those who make a contribution must carry. As one would expect, it is in the least developed countries that the percentage is smallest, and it is there that one individual must push the wheel for many when it comes to producing national power. In the most developed nations one person out of every three or four is a member of the effective population. In the least developed countries the ratio falls to one of ten or eleven (see table 5-2).

It is also worth nothing that when one ranks nations by the size of their effective populations the result is much closer to a ranking by power than was the case when they were ranked by total population size. In other words, population size is an important determinant of national power, but its influence is much more clearly seen when only effective population is considered.

Level of Skills and Economic
Productivity

It is, obviously, not sufficient to assess the relative power of a nation by saying that it has a larger or smaller effective population than does some other state. We must probe further into the relative utility of these individuals as resource-donors to the nation. In particular, we must examine their economic productivity, which in turn reflects both the level of their skills and the capital goods they have at their disposal. The very formulation of effective population as people working in the modern sector of the economy ties the concept of effective population to productivity, but even within the "modern" sector, it is possible to have vast differences in economic productivity. Two nations with roughly equivalent effective populations (e.g., the United States and China) may nevertheless possess widely differing amounts of power thanks to the superior economic productivity of one.

The importance of economic productivity as a source of power is relatively obvious. A productive economy will provide goods that other nations want and a market that other nations seek. It will provide the potential for a mighty military machine, and it will provide its people with a level of wealth that will make them envied and emulated by others. American power has certainly been based in large part upon her wealth, as was the previous power of the European nations that were the first to industrialize.

It would be highly desirable to have an index that would measure the combined effect of size of effective population and level of economic productivity for various nations. No tailor-made index of this kind exists, but the Gross National Product is tolerably close to what we want, and not incidentally, it has proved to be the best generally available measure of national power. GNP reflects both the size of the effective population (including in this instance agricultural workers whose produce is exchanged in the market) and its level of productivity. In addition, it reflects, if only indirectly, the capacity of the economic system to aggregate the output of individuals and groups. Table 5-3 lists the ten nations with the largest GNP's and shows the relation between their rank in GNP, their rank in effective population, and their rank in total population. An examination of these rankings shows clearly that nations registering significantly higher in GNP than they do in total population or in effective population have made up the difference through high economic productivity (for example, Canada and most of the Western European nations). Nations ranking lower in GNP than in total population or in effective population (e.g., China and India) are low in economic productivity and owe their present power in large part to their size.

Aggregation of Individual Contributions

The fourth question to which we must address ourselves in assessing the contribution that population makes to national power is: how effective is the system in aggregating the efforts of the individuals who make up the effective population? We have touched upon the question in mentioning that high economic productivity suggests successful organization and pooling of individual efforts and resources, for it is the system that makes the individual worker productive.

Table 5-3
Power as Indicated by GNP, Total Population, Effective Population

Nation	GNP (billions)[a]	Rank in Total Population[b]	Rank in Effective Population[c]	Rank in GNP
United States	$866	4	2	1
USSR	413	3	3	2
Japan	142	7	5	3
West Germany	133	10	6	4
France	127	13	8	5
United Kingdom	103	11	7	6
China	90	1	1	7
Italy	75	12	9	8
Canada	66	26	13	9
India	43	2	4	10

[a]1968 Gross National Product, United States Arms Control and Disarmament Agency, *World Military Expenditures, 1970* (Washington, D.C.: U.S. Arms Control and Disarmament Agency, 1970), table 2.

[b]Midyear 1968. United Nations, *Demographic Yearbook, 1968* (New York: United Nations, 1969), table 4.

[c]1959-61. For sources, see table 5-2.

But the reference is solely to the capacity of the economic system to aggregate economic resources not to the capacity of the political system to mobilize, organize, and direct individual activities toward political ends. The two capacities differ, and one does not always accompany the other.

In the past it has been widely assumed that economic development and political development proceeded hand in hand. Thus a failure to measure political mobilization directly was not thought overly damaging, for it could be assumed that if a nation possessed a high level of economic productivity it also possessed a high level of political mobilization. The statement is probably true as far as it goes.

The error lies in assuming that low levels of economic productivity and political mobilization are likewise associated. In recent years, we have witnessed repeated examples of nations that experienced a high degree of political mobilization and a corresponding increase in effective population and in national power far in advance of substantial economic modernization. Consider, for example, the wide range of political mobilization exhibited by a group of nondeveloped countries when electoral participation is used as a measure of political mobilization (see table 5-4).

Granted that voting behavior is a somewhat spotty indicator of political mobilization, it is nevertheless interesting to find it varying so greatly in a group

Table 5-4
Political Mobilization and Economic Development

Selected Nondeveloped Countries	Economic Development as Measured by Per Capita GNP	Percentage Voting among People of Voting Age
Guatemala	189	27.5
Albania	175	94.6
Nicaragua	160	92.7
South Korea	144	31.3
Egypt	142	0.0
Indonesia	131	92.0
Liberia	100	82.9
Bolivia	99	51.4
Nigeria	78	40.4
India	73	52.6

Source: All data from Bruce Russet et al., *World Handbook of Political and Social Indicators* (New Haven: Yale University Press, 1964), pp. 84 ff., 195 ff.

of nondeveloped nations. It does not vary this much among the more developed nations. Other indicators support the impression that we are witnessing a new pattern of development in which political mobilization precedes economic modernization rather than following it as it did in the case of the United States and the Western European nations.

In such cases, the usual social and economic indicators will not detect the facts of political life, and the increase in effective population and in national power than such nations experience is likely to be overlooked. Many of the major miscalculations in international politics in recent years and many of the subsequent unexpected outcomes of military confrontations have been at base failures to take into account the increase in power that can be generated simply by developing a political network that mobilizes a peasant population.

China and the Viet Cong are cases in point. China in 1949 was in a state of collapse, exhausted by civil war, her armies disintegrated, a new Communist government just assuming control. A short two years later, Chinese armies entered Korea and fought the greatest power on earth to a military draw. What had changed? Neither population size nor economic productivity had altered significantly. Climate, resources, and area were all the same. What had changed was the political system. For the first time China had a political party and a government bureaucracy that could mobilize a large fraction of the population and commit it to contribute to the war against the United States. Or consider the case of the Viet Cong. Here again the military adversary of the United States is economically backward with low productivity and a traditional social life. In addition, the population is relatively small and the military forces are badly armed, and yet they defy defeat. The only conceivable answer is that the strength of the Viet Cong lies in its political organization, which has succeeded in recruiting a very large proportion of Vietnamese peasants into its effective population. The United States has been slow to recognize the power potential of a politically mobilized effective population in an otherwise backward nation, slow indeed when the consequences have twice been written in American blood.

There is another classic case of the increase in power that accrues to a nation when it uses its political institutions to mobilize new citizens into the effective population. The case is over 180 years old, but it is generally overlooked. We refer to the case of France during the Revolution and the ensuing Napoleonic years, when a sudden burst of power drove France to the mastery of Europe. France was at the time (and had been for years) the most populous nation in Europe except for Russia. She was also relatively rich and well-organized economically. But there seems little question that the French Revolution generated new levels of political mobilization, including the first mass citizen army in history. France's greatly increased effective population seems certain to have played a major role in her sudden acquisition of power.

Some Limitations

In writing of the ways in which population size, economic productivity, and political mobilization contribute to a nation's power, we have perhaps left the impression that national power increases in a linear manner and that a nation can continue to increase its power indefinitely if it continues to enlarge its effective population, raise its productivity, and improve its political mobilization. But this is not the case. There are limits to the increments in power that can be obtained, some of them stemming from the nature of power itself, and some of them stemming from the differential rate and timing of modernization in the various nations of the world.

National power is not a characteristic of the nation but a characteristic of the relationships among nations. It is the relative ability of nations to influence each other in conflicts of interest that concerns us, and here, one nation's gain is another's loss. The power of the United States is not determined solely by its own capacities and skills; it is affected by changes in other nations as well.

The first nations to industrialize gained power rapidly because they left behind their preindustrial rivals. Those next to industrialize gained power relative to those they left behind and also gained on those ahead, who in turn experienced a drop in their relative power. Now new nations are industrializing and gaining in power on the present leaders despite the latter's continued economic modernization. The power gains that a nation achieves through economic modernization do not continue at the same rate after an initial period even if economic development continues at a fast pace. The nation simply grows richer but does not become proportionately more powerful. No one knows exactly where the inflection point on the power curve lies, but there seems little doubt that the power curve flattens out after rising steeply during the early stages of industrialization.

A similar pattern exists as far as political mobilization is concerned. There are obvious gains in power when a nation first expands its political network to incorporate as active participants a sizeable proportion of the national population. The nation whose government can channel its economy, raise and dispose of large tax revenues, count on the informed support of its citizenry, and enlist large armed forces if necessary, will gain rapidly in power over nations that have not yet taken such steps. And it will gain power in catching up with other countries that preceded it. But again the gains are limited by the similar actions of other nations.

One of the authors has written elsewhere of this "power transition":

The result has been that first one nation and then another has experienced a sudden spurt in power. It is like a race in which one runner after another goes into a brief sprint.[6]

Perhaps a race that is also a multidirectional tug-of-war would be a better simile.

There are additional limitations that apply specifically to the capacity of a nation to utilize and to increase its effective population above a certain point. The "nation" is a metaphor for the sum of the individual citizens and groups that compose it. Nations neither make decisions nor take actions. In most nations one specific group, the government, has been assigned the major responsibility for acting in the name of the nation, but the government's success in converting its intentions into actions is dependent upon its ability to mobilize and to utilize various elements of the effective population and the resources that they control.

Government in any system can be considered simply one powerful group among other powerful groups. To the extent that it is *primus inter pares*, it owes its position to the fact that it controls resources and can exercise power over a broader spectrum than other groups. The effective population is also organized into groups that control resources (including their own skills), have extensive networks of relationships, and pursue goals, but usually within a fairly narrowly defined range.

In order to achieve its goals, the government must often seek support from other groups within the effective population. It does this not by mobilizing the entire effective population but rather by forming coalitions with particular groups whose support will be most valuable. To gain this support, the government must be prepared to make concessions, grant favors, or yield resources. Thus, there are costs in mobilizing the effective population.

The most useful coalition partners are, of course, those that control the most resources, and it is precisely these groups that are likely to have the largest number of relationships with others, the greatest complexity of ongoing activities, and the largest number of goals. They are also the groups that require the most resources to carry on their existing programs and to achieve new goals. In order to alter their behavior to distract them from their present activities it may be necessary to reward them heavily. As a general rule it can be said that the greater the potential utility of a coalition partner, the higher the cost that must be borne to win his support. Furthermore, if a group is politically developed, it is likely to have a strong interest in the nature of the government's objectives. If its goals are compatible with those of the government, it is probably efficient to pay even a high price for its support, but if, as is often the case, the group intends in the long run to pursue goals which differ from the government's, then many resources will have to be dissipated in assuring its continued loyalty and support.

It is also possible for the government to obtain support from groups outside the effective population. In doing so, it increases the size of the effective population (i.e., it includes them among those who make a contribution to the realization of national goals), though the level of their effectiveness may remain low. The less skilled and organized the group, the less costly it will be to obtain it as a coalition partner. The problem with such partners is that they are not very useful, for they command few resources beyond their own persons. Perhaps the most frequent use made of noneffectives is as soldiers or, occasionally, as mobs to intimidate effective groups. An appearance of mobilizing mass support is often made by governments, but it often turns out that only a small number of leaders have been mobilized and that they do not in fact control and cannot commit the behavior of their "followers," for the latter have never been tied into any network that would make them members of the effective population.

Viewing the effective population as a resource might make it appear that the larger it is, the better, and that the nation that succeeded in incorporating virtually all of its adult population into the effective population would command maximum power, but it is by no means clear that this is the case. It appears equally probable that there is some optimum level beyond which the effective population becomes dysfunctionally large.

Members of the effective population do not stand by in idle isolation waiting for the government to call for their contribution. They organize themselves into groups and networks and form coalitions of their own in pursuit of their various interests. Their divergent groups compete for scarce resources and fight one another when their goals conflict. Some of these groups becomes so large and so powerful that they compete with, oppose, and occasionally even dominate the national government.

If the effective population is "too large," the government may find that it commands few resources of its own and that its flexibility in making and changing coalitions is thereby decreased. It may also find that its efforts to form successful coalitions are inhibited by internal bickering and factionalism. On the other hand, when the largest and most powerful groups within a highly effective population are unified, it becomes extremely costly for the government to re-direct their activities, so costly that the government may find that it has sur-rendered more in payoffs to its partners than their assistance was worth. Under these circumstances the government will find itself in a position of weakness where it has decreased its ability to achieve its goals.

Shifting Power Patterns

We have said that the power of nations is determined in important measure by the size and effectiveness of their effective populations and that a given nation will experience an increase in its power if it increases its effective population through population growth, economic modernization, or political mobilization. We have also seen that there are limits to the growth in power than can be achieved through any of these means: that population growth beyond a certain rate cannot be absorbed into productive labor but becomes a growth in the dependent population rather than an increase in the effective population; that economic modernization and higher economic productivity beyond a certain point become ways of making the nation richer without producing a commen-surate increase in power; and that political mobilization beyond a certain point produces groups and coalitions that the government has difficulty harnessing for the achievement of national goals. It is not clear in each case whether there is an optimum point of increase beyond which the nation's power actually diminishes or whether there is simply a diminishing return in the power gained, but in either case the power increments gained eventually taper off. Finally, the nations of the world have not all gone through this power transition together but have experienced their greatest gains in power at different times, each gaining in turn at the expense of the others.

Up to this point, we have simply stated these propositions as theoretical generalizations. A brief look at the history of world politics in modern times, however, reveals that this is precisely what has happened. The power stratifica-tion of the international community at any one time, the shifts in that stratifi-cation over time, and the resulting conflicts are clearly traceable to differential changes in effective population.

Let us begin with a consideration of international stratification. It is cus-tomary today to divide the world into strata as developed, developing, and less developed nations. (The last term is pejorative, and is constantly changed to avoid offense. It has progressed from "backward" to "underdeveloped" to "non-developed" to "less developed" or even "developing" though this last term seems better applied to a middle strata.) These are not simply descriptions of economic development, though they are often phrased as such, but refer also to political and social structures. In addition, they characterize to some extent a power status, for ever since the Industrial Revolution the world has been domi-nated by the developed nations.

As a group, the developed nations have all enjoyed marked advantages over the presently less developed nations, both in their present position and in the ease with which they achieved it:

1. They were the first to industrialize and had the advantage of increasing their effective populations rapidly while the rest of the world "stood still" (or developed much less rapidly).
2. With the notable exception of Japan, they began their industrialization at a point where they already had a higher level of economic productivity and a lower rate of population increase than the less developed nations have today, thus facilitating the absorption of new millions into the effective population.
3. Population growth and economic growth were rapid as development proceeded and these nations passed from nonindustrial to industrial status. (France was an interesting exception in regard to population growth).
4. Rapid growth was sustained for a considerable period of time.

Simon Kuznets has described the resulting gap between the developed and the less developed strata:

In general, over the last century to century and a half per capita product grew much more rapidly in the presently developed countries; and since they, with the single exception of Japan, entered on modern growth with per capita product already well above that of the less developed countries today, these international differences must have widened. And the rapidity with which they widened was largely a function of the unusually high growth rates in the developed countries.

But, until very recent decades, population also tended to grow more rapidly in the developed countries (except for France) than in the less developed. This meant that both per capita and total product grew at much higher rates in the developed countries—and relative economic magnitudes shifted in favor of that group.[7]

This gap in economic efficiency and in power between the developed and the less developed strata made it possible for the developed nations to conquer and to dominate the less developed countries, first through colonial rule and more recently through subtler forms of economic and political domination. The result has been to impede still further the development of these nations, for their overlords and "senior partners" have shaped their economies to serve their own ends and have used their power to encourage rulers who will not disturb the status quo.

Thus the presently underdeveloped areas (and they are, indeed, underdeveloped) face many handicaps as they undertake to modernize, to increase their effective populations, and to go through their own power transition. They start late, from an economically poorer position, and under the political domination of others. They differ from their European predecessors in that many of them have undergone considerable political modernization and effected considerable political mobilization even in advance of economic modernization. This would appear to offer an advantage, but it also has brought problems in that it has helped to place these nations in a demographically poor position to increase their effective populations.

This last point requires some explanation. Fertility and mortality respond to different environmental stimuli. Fertility patterns are influenced by widely shared social values and are implemented by repeated individual choices. Changes in social values are not easily brought about by governmental action, and the high fertility characteristic of most peasant societies does not drop sharply (at least this has been the historical experience up to now) until economic modernization and urbanization with their accompanying life styles are well advanced.

Mortality, on the other hand, is more likely to change in response to structural changes within the society. When governments establish sanitary facilities, institute health programs, or reorganize food distribution, the effects upon mortality are immediate. Political modernization, then, may have an immediate, visible effect upon mortality, but it is unlikely to have as direct an effect upon fertility.

It is demographically significant, therefore, which pattern of modernization a nation pursues. In Western Europe and in the United States, economic and social modernization had been sustained for a considerable period before political modernization and accompanying governmental programs brought a significant reduction in mortality. Thus fertility and mortality rates dropped together, with a gap between them large enough to assure substantial population growth but not so large that the growth could not be absorbed into the effective population.

The presently developing world is pursuing a different course. Relatively high levels of political modernization are bringing governmental programs that reduce mortality, while the peasant economy and social system remain relatively intact. The result is low mortality combined with high fertility, producing the contemporary population explosion. Such rapid population growth coming in advance of economic modernization disturbs the delicate balance of economic and demographic factors that is required to produce a larger effective population.

The current stratification of the international community into levels of economic development and the resulting domination by the most developed nations are directly related to differential mobilization of the effective population. So too are the shifts of power within the top group of nations.

Kuznets has described the varying rates of development within the group of the most developed nations:

The interesting aspect is that the same rapid shifts in economic magnitude, caused by wide differences in the growth rates of per capita product population, and total product, are found *within* the group of developed countries. Despite the fairly high rates of growth of per capita product over long periods in all developed countries, usually well above 10 per cent per decade, and despite the impressive rates of population growth in most of these countries, these rates and those for total product differed widely among the countries themselves. Consequently, over the long periods, there were drastic shifts in relative economic magnitude.[8]

In other words, these nations all developed by increasing their economic productivity, their population size (and their political mobilization as well). All increased their effective populations, *but they did not do so at the same rate or at the same time*. Using per capita Gross Domestic Product as an indicator, figure 5-1 shows the changes that have occurred in economic productivity in a number of nations over the years. Figure 5-2 shows changes in total output (total Gross Product). GDP, like GNP, gives a rough indication of the combined effect of size

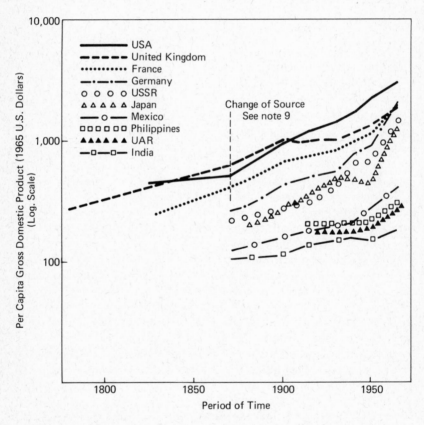

Figure 5-1. Changes in Economic Productivity (Per Capita Gross Domestic Product).

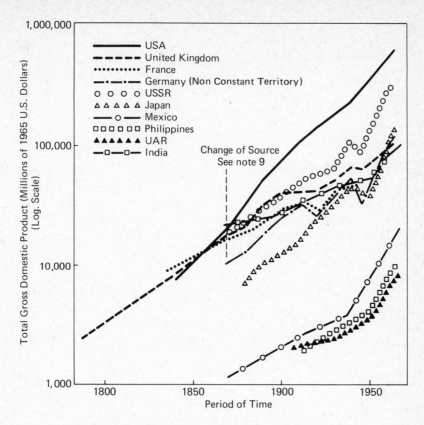

Figure 5-2. Changes in Total Economic Output.

of effective population and level of economic productivity. It also approximates an indicator of relative national power.

Figure 5-1 shows the distinct stratification of developed versus nondeveloped nations in terms of economic productivity. Figure 5-2 shows that they are also stratified in power, though India's extremely large population lifts her into the upper group. (The logarithmic scale distorts the magnitude of differences but is necessary if such a range of differences is to be encompassed in a single graph.)

The figures also show how nations pass each other due to their varying rates of development and how even rapidly rising economic productivity is not sufficient to guarantee a nation world leadership if it is forced to compete with larger nations that are also modernizing. Recent history is encapsulated as Britain passes France and both are passed by the United States and the Soviet Union. Germany's challenge to Britain and France is also suggested.

Patterns of Conflict

The political consequences of these shifts in power are highly significant. More than any other factor, they explain the underlying reasons for world conflict.

At any given period, the most powerful nation heads an international order that includes some of the powers of secondary importance and also some minor nations and dependencies. In recent history, the dominant nation has always been a large industrial nation whose economic and political modernization have provided it with the largest highly effective population. As additional large nations industrialize, the old leader is challenged, for the distribution of wealth and privilege is no longer coincident with the distribution of power. If change cannot be effected peaceably, the challenger may turn to military conflict to achieve its goals. It may seek to dominate the existing world order (as in the German threat that culminated in World War I) or it may seek to establish a rival international order (as in the case of the Soviet challenge today).

If the distribution of power among nations remained the same for centuries, the powerful would eventually shape the world to their liking and there would be perpetual peace (though not perhaps justice). It is when power shifts that the peace is broken, for then power passes to the dissatisfied who will use force, if necessary, to change the status quo.[10]

The danger of war is greatest, not at the moment when one great nation catches up with another in power, but rather in the years just before that point is reached. Perceptions and misperceptions play an important role here, for it is at this period that each side is most likely to miscalculate the power of the other. A challenger that has risen rapidly may easily become infatuated with its own new strength and overestimate its ability to defeat its rivals. Nazi Germany made such an error and so did Imperial Japan. A dominant nation, used to the privileges of power, may fail to make any accommodation to the needs of a new rival and may either minimize the threat or overreact when a new challenger begins to assert itself. The United States has exhibited both attitudes in regard to Nazi Germany and the Soviet Union.

Miscalculation is commonplace where a nation has gained in power through internal developments rather than external aggression, and underestimation of a nation's power is particularly likely when the basis for increased power lies in the political mobilization of new effective population, for which we have no measure, rather than in increased economic wealth, which the modern world calculates so closely.

There is perhaps no way that a dominant nation can guarantee its preponderance indefinitely in the face of larger modernizing challengers, but an accurate understanding of the mainsprings of power will maximize its power and security.

Notes

1. Katherine and A.F.K. Organski, *Population and World Power* (New York: Alfred A. Knopf, 1961), pp. 3-4.

2. A.F.K. Organski, "Effective Population as a Source of International Power" in Machael Louw (ed.), *International Aspects of Overpopulation* (London: MacMillan, 1972).

3. United Nations, *Statistical Yearbook 1970* (New York: United Nations, 1971), table 18.

4. United States Census Bureau, *Statistical Abstract of the United States, 1971* (Washington, D.C., 1971), p. 364.

5. United States Treasury Department, Internal Revenue Service, *Statistics of Incomes, 1968, Individual Income Tax Returns*, table 8A, p. 194.

6. A.F.K. Organski, *World Politics*, 2nd ed. (New York: Alfred A. Knopf, 1968), p. 344.

7. Simon Kuznets, *The Economic Growth of Nations* (Cambridge: Belknap Press of the Harvard University Press, 1971), p. 34.

8. Ibid.

9. Adjusted Gross Domestic Product data prior to 1870 for France, the United Kingdom, and the United States: Simon Kuznets, *The Economic Growth of Nations* (n. 7), table 1, pp. 11-15.

After 1870 estimate of Gross Domestic Product data for India, Mexico, Philippines and UAR: Angus Maddison, *Economic Progress and Policy in Developing Countries* (London: Allen and Unwin, 1970), tables b-1 and b-2, pp. 299-301.

Estimate of Gross Domestic Product data for remaining countries: Angus Maddison, *Economic Growth in Japan and the USSR* (London: Allen and Unwin, 1969), table b-1, pp. 154-55 and Bureau of Census, U.S. Dept. of Commerce, *Long-Term Economic Growth* (Washington, D.C.: U.S. Government Printing Office, 1966), series d-1 through d-7, pp. 249-51. These series are for the Gross National Product, and we assume they move consistently with the Gross Domestic Product. A constant dollar base at factor cost converted to U.S. 1965 relative prices was obtained for all countries from Maddison's, *Economic Progress*, table a-11, p. 295.

Population estimates for India, Mexico, Philippines, and UAR, ibid., table c-1, p. 303.

Population estimates for other countries: Bureau of Census, U.S. Department of Commerce, *Long-Term Economic Growth*, series d41-d50, pp. 254-256 and Arthur S. Banks, *Cross-Polity Time-Series Data* (Cambridge: The MIT Press, 1971), segment 1, pp. 3-35.

Adjustments were made to German data to compensate for territorial loss, using Angus Maddison, *Economic Growth in the West* (The Twentieth

Century Fund, 1964), table a-1, p. 195; all other estimates are based on constant territory.

The minimal time interval used in the plotting of the data is ten years whenever data availability permits.

10. Katherine and A.F.K. Organski (n. 1), p. 244.

6

The Political Environment of Population Control in India and Pakistan

Jason L. Finkle

Governments throughout the world have only recently begun to view population size and population growth as appropriate issues for public policy determination. The developing nations, starting in the 1960s, were the first to confront rapid population growth as a national problem that might be ameliorated by government intervention. Before then, to the extent that population was considered as a factor in the development equation, it was generally regarded as of secondary importance and looked upon as a problem that would diminish in time as a result of other social changes, particularly economic growth. The economic frustrations and disappointments of the 1950s and 1960s did much to change this perspective. Development-oriented politicians and administrators began to recognize that rapid population growth was not merely an ephemeral problem but a major and potentially enduring obstacle to modernization.

India was the first nation in the world to react to the implications of population growth by designating family planning as a national policy aimed at reducing the birth rate. Although family planning was being encouraged by voluntary associations in Pakistan during the 1950s, it was not until 1960—almost a decade after India—that the government of Pakistan made fertility control a matter of public policy. For both countries, the formulation of a population policy was merely a first step in a long and difficult process of social change intended to alter fertility behavior. Despite the relatively early commitment of the two governments to family planning, both nations only began to translate earlier policy pronouncements into serious programmatic activities in 1965, when a series of demographic, political, and technological developments converged to provide a new impetus to family planning.

First, better demographic data revealed that the rate of population growth in India and Pakistan was higher than either country had realized. The Indian

The basic analysis contained in this chapter was developed by the author in 1968 before the political events which led to the forced resignation of President Ayub Khan. Although it does take some account of the post-Ayub period, it does not attempt to consider the implications for family planning of the political separation of East and West Pakistan.

An earlier version of this chapter appeared under the title "Politics, Development Strategy, and Family Planning Programs in India and Pakistan," in *Journal of Comparative Administration* 3, no. 3 (November 1971), pp. 259-295. The present chapter has benefited from the comments and criticisms of my colleagues at the Center for Population Planning of the University of Michigan.

census of 1961 showed that population growth during the preceding decade was 30 million more than had been expected.[1] In Pakistan, not only had the population grown beyond expectations, but the real growth rate in all probability exceeded the figure indicated in the 1961 census.[2] Second, donor nations and international agencies began urging the two countries to devote greater resources to curtailing fertility and indicated their willingness to provide technical and financial assistance to that end.[3] International concern was expressed over the quality of family planning activity in the two countries, lending support to those groups in India and Pakistan who were already stressing the importance of population as a factor in economic development. Third, no development was more significant than the introduction of a new contraceptive technology known as the intrauterine contraceptive device (IUD).

For years those concerned with rapid population growth and the need for family planning had been looking for a contraceptive that was easily administered, inexpensive, reversible, medically safe, and that did not require daily or repeated action on the part of the user.[4] Many believed the IUD possessed more of the characteristics of an ideal contraceptive than any method previously available. It was regarded as particularly appropriate for the developing nations where the lack of medical personnel, inadequate distribution systems, and weak motivation on the part of potential users magnified the liabilities of conventional contraceptives.[5]

Prior to its adoption by the Indian and Pakistani family planning programs, the IUD had been tried on an experimental basis in numerous countries. The extensive reports and statistical analyses of its effectiveness, acceptance, and side effects were favorable.[6] Although subsequent experience indicated that the IUD was somewhat less than the "ideal" contraceptive and possessed its own inherent liabilities, family planning leaders—including medical doctors—did not anticipate the programmatic consequences of the IUD's deficiencies, even though there was evidence of these deficiencies in the period of experimentation.[7]

Paradoxically, this failure to fully anticipate the manifold problems with the IUD may have aided the cause of family planning in India and Pakistan. In development planning there is a tendency of people to undertake projects "because of the erroneously presumed *absence* of a challenge, because the task looks easier and more manageable than it will turn out to be."[8] This "principle of the hiding hand," as Hirschman calls it, explains much about the response of India and Pakistan to the IUD. For the first time, the two countries approached the population question confident that they possessed a technology that was suitable in sociological, medical, and organizational terms. They set optimistic goals of fertility reduction, made population policy a prominent feature of their development objectives, and increased the resources and authority of their family planning organizations. When it was later realized that the IUD was not the ideal contraceptive that would enable the two countries to curtail fertility rates as rapidly as hoped, each country was in a sense saddled with its own policy pronouncements, publicized goals, and family planning organizations. It was then too late to withdraw gracefully from these commitments, and each country had to pursue its own goals with imperfect contraceptive technologies. It is therefore possible to conclude, as Hirschman might, that if the IUD had not raised such high hopes, neither India nor Pakistan would have invested the level of resources and manpower in family planning that it did.

Within a few years there was mounting evidence that Pakistan had been more effective than India in delivering family planning services. From the outset in 1965, when both countries seriously organized to tackle the population problem, Pakistan placed greater stress on promoting the IUD. Even when Pakistan subsequently introduced sterilization into its family planning program—a method of birth prevention long familiar to the Indian program—it became evident that Pakistan would have a higher rate of acceptance than India in this program area also. The comparatively superior performance of Pakistan in family planning was accomplished, moreover, without the advantages that might be expected to explain performance variation between national family planning programs. In fact, the variables that would be most likely to have predictive value favored India: India had a head start of several years in its family planning program; it had more and better trained doctors, administrators, and technical personnel to carry out its program; it had a more extensive and highly developed health system, including local clinics, through which to reach its target population; and finally, the Indian population seemed more sociologically "ready" to adopt measures of fertility control.[9]

Comparative Performance

Before analyzing the reasons for the performance differential between the Indian and Pakistani programs, we must give some attention to the problems of measuring and comparing family planning programs. As in all organized efforts at social change, there are many technical problems (and disputes) regarding appropriate measurement criteria and methodology. In the area of family planning, these problems are compounded by inferior data and the recency of most programs. Yet comparative performance is the quantitative basis for understanding policy and program developments in the two countries. Additionally, it constitutes the empirical point of departure for much of the analysis which follows.

Numerous criteria have been utilized to evaluate family planning programs ranging from a count of the number of personnel trained to the number of client-contacts made by family planning field workers.[10] The suitability of any set of evaluative criteria, of course, depends upon precisely what is being measured or evaluated. For example, the number of family planning posters or circulars distributed does not provide a scientific basis for assessing the effectiveness of a communications effort in changing attitudes toward family size and contraception. In the absence, however, of extensive surveys of family planning knowledge, attitudes, and practice, an assessment of the diffusion of posters and circulars constitutes one index, albeit crude, of the degree of activity of those responsible for communicating information about family planning.

Ideally, the most appropriate as well as significant criterion for evaluating a family planning program would be its demographic impact in reducing the fertility rate, i.e., the number of births which the program has prevented. Although several notable attempts have been made to determine births prevented as a consequence of family planning programs, there is no consensus on which approach to the question is most valid.[11] Furthermore, without information about the age, parity, and prior contraceptive practices of the adopter as well as the retention rates of the IUD, it is impossible for any of these approaches to accurately assess the demographic impact of a family planning program.[12] Neither the Indian nor the Pakistani program invested sufficient resources to gather these requisite data on a systematic basis. Therefore, in view of the methodological issue and lack of proper data, the number of acceptors as indicated by IUD insertions and sterilizations may be the most reliable and appropriate measures of program effectiveness.

As a criterion of relative administrative effectiveness, utilization of these intermediate indicators rather than estimates of births prevented seems justifiable for several other reasons. First, the major organizational efforts of both programs in the years under examination were focused primarily on IUD insertions and sterilizations. Second, the family planning administrators themselves largely ignored questions concerning the characteristics of the acceptors and the demographic consequences of the program. The Pakistani program under Commissioner Enver Adil, in the view of his successor, concentrated excessively on " 'input' targets—such things as insertions, supplies, and personnel activities," rather than the ultimate 'output' goals of fertility limitation.[13] John Lewis makes a similar criticism of the Indian program: "The effort began very quickly after its launching in 1965 to project a pervasive image of sub-targetism. . . . The system developed an almost manic focus on near-term achievement."[14] Finally, the fragmentary evidence that exists concerning demographic impact of the two programs as well as the opinions of those who have observed both programs first-hand do not challenge the appropriateness of the intermediate indicators— IUD insertions and sterilizations—as being roughly representative of the relative accomplishments of India and Pakistan in family planning.[15]

The comparison of the two programs shown in figures 6-1 and 6-2 is based on the yearly number of IUD insertions and sterilization operations standardized to a rate per 1000 total population for each country. As indicated graphically in figure 6-1, India first introduced the IUD into its family planning program in 1965. After a promising start, the Indian program leveled off and soon began to decline. Peak monthly performance for IUD acceptance occurred from October, 1965 to March, 1966, during which time an average of about 100,000 insertions

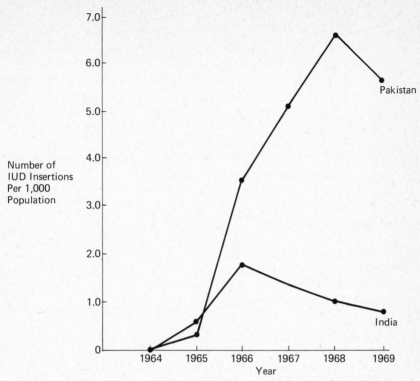

Figure 6-1. Number of IUD Insertions Per 1,000 Population in India and Pakistan: 1964-69. Source: Derived from data contained in Dorothy Nortman, "Population and Family Planning Programs: A Factbook," *Reports on Population/Family Planning*, no. 2 (New York: Population Council, 1971), p. 34. Calculations are based on 1969 population figures of 131.6 million for Pakistan and 536.9 million for India (*1969 World Population Data Sheet*, Population Reference Bureau).

took place each month. Since then, however, the IUD adoption rate gradually but consistently went down, and by 1970 the monthly average was about 40,000 insertions for an approximate yearly rate of .8 insertions per 1000 population.[16]

The operational stage of Pakistan's IUD program started about six months after India had launched its IUD effort. Notwithstanding India's brief lead during 1965, Pakistan experienced a consistently higher annual rate of IUD insertions (see figure 6-1). By April 1970, its cumulative rate of insertions was 22.4 per 1000—more than three and one-half times the rate the Indian program had achieved. The magnitude of this difference may be partially attributed to Pakistan's choice of the IUD as its primary contraceptive technology. While India stressed the IUD, most family planning centers continued to employ a limited

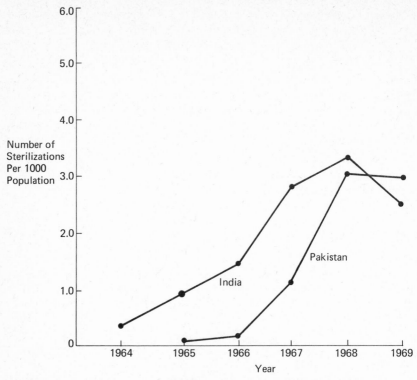

Figure 6-2. Number of Sterilizations Per 1,000 Population in India and Pakistan: 1964–69. Source: Derived from data contained in Dorothy Nortman, "Population and Family Planning Programs: A Factbook," *Reports on Population/Family Planning*, no. 2 (New York: Population Council, 1971), p. 37. Calculations are based on 1969 population figures of 131.6 million for Pakistan and 536.9 million for India (*1969 World Population Data Sheet*, Population Reference Bureau).

"cafeteria approach" whereby health personnel or patients had some choice in contraceptive method.

The sterilization performance of the two countries as shown in figure 6-2 reveals a pattern which challenges the assumption that Pakistan's success with the IUD was simply a result of concentrating its resources in one technology. Sterilization as a form of fertility control was introduced into the Indian national family planning strategy as early as 1957 in some parts of the country. The yearly acceptance rate of sterilization, as well as the cumulative rate, had not climbed beyond one per 1000 by 1964. Sterilization was given greater emphasis, however, in the revitalized family planning program of 1965, and its importance as a contraceptive technology continued to increase during the next four years. In 1968 India had achieved its highest yearly rate of 3.4 sterilizations per 1000 (mainly male sterilizations, or vasectomy).

Pakistan, on the other hand, did not begin to perform sterilizations until 1966, and then only on a very limited basis. Family planning leaders in Pakistan had mistakenly assumed that sterilization was not an acceptable method of fertility control in Muslim Pakistan, and they were therefore reluctant to give it programmatic emphasis. The level of performance after one year of experience with sterilization in Pakistan was so low that by the end of the year the rate of acceptance was still below that attained by India nine years earlier. In a turn of events unanticipated by program administrators in Pakistan, sterilization acceptance rates in East Pakistan showed a marked upward surge. This phenomenon— in which West Pakistan participated only belatedly and to a much lesser extent— resulted in a level of monthly performance in Pakistan during the latter half of 1968 equal to the sterilization rate of India. In less than four years, the yearly sterilization rate of Pakistan was comparable to India's rate.

In summary, India had a head start in its sterilization program, but after 1969, Pakistan experienced nearly the same annual number of sterilizations per 1000 population. Within a few months after the inception of IUD programs in both countries, Pakistan began to exhibit a consistently higher level of performance. When performance rates for both IUD's and sterilizations are combined, Pakistan achieved an annual rate in 1969 of 8.62 acceptors per 1000 population, compared to a combined annual rate of 3.34 per 1000 in India.

What explains the more impressive performance of the Pakistan program? It has already been suggested that the answer is not found in the sociological character of the population, the technical or administrative abilities of program personnel, or the program inputs. The search for an answer to the reasons for the family planning performance differential between India and Pakistan might start with the more general observation that from the mid-1960s until 1969, when President Ayub of Pakistan was forced to resign, Pakistan compiled a more impressive record than India in its rate of economic growth and in most economic development programs.[17] One hypothesis would be that Pakistan managed to move into a more favorable "development orbit," whereby success in one endeavor contributed to success in other related fields.

A more significant observation is that Pakistan's sharp improvement in programs associated with economic growth also followed a dramatic change in the character of its political system in 1958. The political transformation of the country was a powerful influence in its subsequent surge in economic and development activity. The major theme of the present analysis is that the properties of the political systems of India and Pakistan also had important consequences for comparative performance of their family planning programs. The most important political features that seemed to impinge on the comparative performance of the two family planning programs were: (a) the degree to which political power was centralized; (b) the proximity of planners and technocrats to the political leadership; (c) the existence of multiple or alternative centers of political power, especially politically influential subunits of government and private associations; and (d) the development strategies adopted by the political system and its capacity to implement them. The implicit assumption is that the effective implementation of development programs, including family planning, depends in large measure on nonprogrammatic factors external to the specific organization charged with responsibility for program management.

Politics, Development Strategy, and Family Planning

The pervasive sense of scarcity in India and Pakistan serves as a constant reminder to politicians, planners, and bureaucrats that without economic growth the eloquently expressed ideals and aspirations of their leaders will remain beyond reach of the people. Reflecting this need, the five-year plan of each country has set forth a series of development goals and has spelled out economic programs and policies designed to achieve them. While there have been differences between the two countries regarding specific goals, investment allocations, and rates of growth to be achieved, the major differences in development strategy between India and Pakistan have been largely a result of the planning *process* and the political context of planning in each country.

Policy formulation in India is subject to the restraints and demands of diverse groups and elements in the society. Economic plans and goals are tempered by the intervention of the political sector, which is concerned with values other than economic growth, such as social welfare and more equal distribution of wealth. In effect, economic planning in India is politicized; it is subject to much of the same public scrutiny, debate, bargaining, and compromise that characterize Indian politics in general. While the Indian government makes no pretense that planning decisions are made by popular referendum, it has not attempted to insulate the planning process from the pressures of democratic political life. A.H. Hanson, an astute analyst of Indian planning, confirms this view:

The techniques of planning that the [Planning] Commission employs, which involve wide consultation and extensive publicity, provide opportunities for the effective exertion of a variety of organized pressures. This is advantageous to the extent that the pressures can be absorbed, or that the people exerting them can be persuaded to accept compromises. It is disadvantageous to the extent that the Commission is compelled to diverge from economic rationality, to raise hopes doomed to frustration, and to seek fictitious 'agreement'. . . . Both the advantages and disadvantages, however, are the essence of any planning in a political order based on conciliation.[18]

The Indian political system has held together despite the severity of its nation-building crises because the central government has recognized its own limitations and has not strained its capacity to mobilize for development at the risk of violating or alienating major segments of the society. State governments, parliamentary bodies, and opposition parties must be reckoned with in the formulation of economic plans and development strategy. India's prime minister has been compelled to accept these restraints in those instances where development plans must be sacrificed or modified. This, in part, explains the continued legitimacy accorded the Indian political system by its people as well as the rate and direction of Indian development.

Pakistan's development strategy and the process by which it is formulated is also an expression of the country's politics and influence patterns. But politics and the distribution of influence in Pakistan differ from India. Khalid B. Sayeed has characterized Pakistan's political system under General Ayub Khan as a constitutional autocracy:

Ever since he seized power, he has consistently argued that parliamentary democracy is not likely to work in Pakistan where literacy is so low and where the people are not informed or mature enough to use their votes to support certain national policies or programs. [19]

As a consequence of Ayub's low assessment of parliamentary democracy and his power to translate his ideas into action, Pakistan's political system came to be comprised of a strong executive, weak parliament, and weak provinces vis-à-vis the central government. The political order muffled rather than facilitated the articulation of political demands, and the leadership was committed to achieving national development goals without great regard for ideological considerations or popular sentiments.

General Ayub's seizure of power in 1958 signified for many that for the first time Pakistan had a political leader strong enough to get things done, or, as Ayub himself phrased it, "to clear up the mess."[20] His task of providing Pakistan with firm political leadership and moving the nation into a more promising development orbit was facilitated by the nation's political chaos, the pervasiveness of economic stagnation, and the endemic dissatisfaction of the population. In reviewing the state of affairs in 1958, Gustav Papanek states that the new government "was sure of a long lease on political life . . . [and] was strong enough to carry out policies that offended particular groups and were unpopular in the short run."[21]

Although Ayub sought to create a basis of legitimacy for his seizure of power through a new constitution and a popular election, the real basis of his support was mass disenchantment with the old regime and the hopes his leadership inspired. The takeover in 1958 was seen as a classic case of military intervention by a modernizing military elite, led and epitomized by General Ayub. At a minimum, "military modernizers" are expected to effect orderly change and manage the affairs of the nation in a way conducive to modernization. The basis of legitimacy for Ayub, then, depended upon what Lipset has called effectiveness, and the meaning of effectiveness in most developing nations is economic growth.[22]

The new government under Ayub had no ready-made development strategy, but it did possess sufficient political strength to assure itself an opportunity to learn from its own mistakes and to identify domestic and foreign talent that might enable it to energize the nation's economy. "The government," in the words of Papanek, "made economic policy a central concern, since it had justified its takeover largely in terms of economic mismanagement by previous governments."[23] In the candid language of one of the government's former chief economists, Mahbub-ul-Haq, Pakistan

took the basic decision of devoting all the energies of the system towards a faster pace of economic development and to forget about the issues of more equitable distribution or a more democratic system of economic organization. The first priority was growth; the other questions will come later.[24]

If India's development strategy could be described as more or less politicized, then it is appropriate to describe Pakistan's as "depoliticized." Pakistan was able to adopt a development strategy that subordinated—if not ignored—questions of social welfare, distribution, and equity to the primary objective of rapid economic growth. This was possible because the process of planning and economic policy formulation did not occur in a political arena where organized groups and political parties concerned about such issues as distribution and equity had access or influence. In the words of the economist Haq, "The Planning Commission was isolated from the political process—its only mandate being to devise policy for yet a faster growth rate."[25] It would be more accurate to postulate that planning was insulated from the free play of group politics or from the democratic political process. If large industrialists, landowners, and entrepreneurs did not influence economic decisions and plans directly, it was because they found those plans congenial to their interests or they had access to other, less overt channels of influence.[26]

To the extent that a planning commission is expected to coordinate economic development efforts, it requires, perhaps more than any other agency of government, the active support of the dominant political leadership. Unless the planning commission occupies a special place in government close to the nexus of political power, it will be handicapped in attempting to coordinate development and diffuse a developmental orientation among the various governmental programs.[27] It would be hard to argue that India's Planning Commission was *less* interested in economic development than Pakistan's, although it certainly possessed a broader or more balanced view of development. What made the Pakistani Planning Commission a more effective agent of economic growth—whose influence was felt in family planning as well as numerous other economic programs—was the comparatively greater enthusiasm and support enjoyed by the commission from Pakistan's political leaders and the closeness of the relationship between the planners and President Ayub.[28] While there have been times since independence when India's Planning Commission had much political support and influence, in more recent years its political support has dwindled and its influence has diminished. It has become one agency among many competing for the attention of national leaders.[29]

Under the Ayub government, Pakistan adopted policies and organized programs designed to accelerate economic growth, and, in contrast to India at that time, selected the type of industrial investment that has a much shorter gestation period and a much lower capital-output ratio.[30] As the Ayub government formulated its policy for long-range economic growth, it took cognizance of population factors. In 1959 Ayub had declared that "the menace of overpopulation and rapid rate of population increase exists in most underdeveloped countries, and a big concentrated drive is necessary to educate the people about the evils of overpopulation."[31] Within a few years the government considered population control as an essential ingredient of its economic policy. Population control was approached with the same determination and energy that characterized Pakistan's other economic programs.

With the active support of President Ayub, Pakistan's family planning program from 1965 was vested with the power to by-pass or ignore many of the conventional political, administrative, and social restraints that impede family planning programs in other nations. The major responsibility of the family planning program in Pakistan was managerial, a difficult responsibility, yet one that was restricted largely to developing an effective system to promote and deliver contraceptives to potential adopters. Under Ayub the program enjoyed the direct and personal attention of the president, who made frequent references to family planning in public statements. More important, he also would scrutinize monthly reports of the program's progress and return them to administrators with his comments.[32] With the support of the President, reinforced by Pakistan's planners and technicians, the program was able to use its time, energy, and resources to train personnel and to improve its logistics, its supply system, and its evaluation system. In addition, it had the authority and funds to provide incentive payments over and above normal salaries to government servants as well as others who in various ways rendered services to the program.

India's political leadership did not show the same level of support for family planning as evidenced by Ayub, partly because economic growth, population control, and other developmental programs in India have been viewed as subordinate to the larger efforts of nation building.[33] Population control in India had neither the strong political constituency nor the autocratic executive leadership which would have been necessary to give it the dynamism of Pakistan's family planning program.

The Indian program was not permitted to confine itself to the delivery of service. While they certainly did not ignore this central role, the program leaders were not able to pursue it with the singlemindedness of purpose of the Pakistani program. They were required to invest much of their time, energy, and resources in winning over other authoritative institutions within India. Program managers in the central government had to deal with reluctant states headed by chief ministers, finance ministers, or health ministers who did not necessarily attach a high priority to family planning. The leaders of the Indian family planning program had to convince various voluntary associations, regional groups, caste groups, economic interests, religious groups, and professional organizations that the family planning program, and fertility control itself, would not undermine their relative power, status, and economic position in the society. For example, Pakistan was able to employ women to insert the IUD after a relatively brief training period, a practice which did not evoke mass opposition from Pakistan's medical association. Pakistan's doctors do not have an independent medical association with the organized strength of the Indian medical association nor would the Pakistan government have been predisposed to respond to their influence. The contrasting sensitivity of the Indian government to significant groups within its own polity largely precluded the family planning program from violating the professional norms of the medical profession by employing paramedical personnel for similar roles except on an experimental basis.

The task of eliciting the cooperation and support of authoritative institutions and state and local political leaders in India was made more difficult due to the lack of strong political support at the national level. The meager political support given to family planning in India is partly a result of the fact that India's Planning Commission simply did not have the political impact that characterized the counterpart unit in Pakistan. Still, many issues without the endorsement of the Planning Commission receive intense support from the political sector in India. It appears, however, that family planning has inherent qualities which make it something less than an attractive cause to politicians dependent on a mass electorate in a peasant society.

Population control may have great appeal to planners, intellectuals, and that select group of the populace who see the connection between population growth and development, but in India, as in most societies, the short run, parochial political rewards of family planning are negligible, and, in some cases, are outweighed by the political risks and liabilities. Although government investment in family planning programs in the developing nations may have a higher rate of return than any other investment available to government, the benefits from a national family planning program are long range, hard to demonstrate (except in statistical terms), and generally devoid of the visible impact of a new bridge or road in a community. A politician or an administrator has little prospect of receiving acclaim from his constituents for helping to prevent the birth of X number of Indian or Pakistani children. Without inherent political appeal and without being able to count on the continued and active support of political leaders, Indian family planning administrators have had to devote organizational resources to gaining the cooperation and support of governmental units and groups rather than delivering services.

The political systems of India and Pakistan and their divergent approaches to development were reflected in their family planning programs. The programs' goals, organizational structures, and administrative relationships differed, not because one country possessed a more incisive appreciation of the elements of family planning "success," but because the political environment in each country imposed distinct demands on the family planning organization.

India

As early as 1962, during the period of the Third Five-Year Plan, India announced that a goal of its family planning program was to reduce the birth rate from an official 41 per 1000 to 25 per 1000 within ten years.[34] During the Third Plan, more money and resources were made available to the family planning effort; yet, despite the impressive increase in expenditures over the previous plan period, actual expenditures remained below 50 percent of the budgetary allocation for family planning.[35] Several factors have contributed to underspending in the Indian family planning program, including the questionably ambitious goals of the program itself.

Among India's many competent demographers, statisticians, and planners, it has been almost openly acknowledged that the family planning target was beyond the capacity of the program. Ambitious goals are not necessarily bad, but the effect of the family planning target was to deny the program realistic objectives which could constitute the basis for detailed plans of action at various program levels. Field administrators tacitly ignored the government's targets, and in a number of states the targets were openly rejected and reformulated by the states themselves. The process of target-setting in the Indian family planning program gave primacy to those enthusiasts whose aspirations were intended to please the country's political leaders and impress foreign donors. The more sophisticated judgment of India's many competent planners who understood the relationship between resources and goals was not taken into account. Thus, five years later, under the Fourth Five-Year Plan, the target was to reduce the birth rate from 41 to 23 within a ten year period, a reflection of the continuing lack of realism in the program's goals.[36]

Even before the Fourth Plan, there was a general recognition that the Indian family planning program was seriously inadequate and required reorganization.[37] The introduction of the IUD provided an uncommon opportunity to change the program. The kinds of organizational modifications required to improve the program, however, also necessitated the cooperation of India's bureaucracy as well as that of the states. The justification for change may have been compelling, but the Indian bureaucracy demonstrated a deep aversion to internal changes, and the Indian states were not inclined to relinquish their jealously guarded powers, especially for the cause of family planning. In the absence of active interest and support from the political sector, recommended organizational changes were only partially implemented by the center as well as the states.

Perhaps the most important organizational decision made by the Indian government relative to family planning in this period was to perpetuate its designation as a "health" subject, a determination which has had far reaching implications for the Indian program up to the present time. Although the policy impetus for family planning in India grew out of concern over the effect of rapid population growth on economic development, early family planning efforts were associated with the provision of health care for mothers and children. Among the responsibilities of a Maternal and Child Health Service was providing family planning advice, usually only upon request. When the government of India decided to increase its level of activity in family planning in the mid-1960s, it simply followed convention by treating family planning as another aspect of health. An alternative choice could have been made at that time, but it was politically and administratively convenient to leave family planning under health.

The decision to regard family planning as a health subject had three major consequences affecting the strategy, structure, and performance of the Indian program: (1) responsibility for the program was vested in the Ministry of Health; (2) control over vital aspects of the program was retained by the states, who have constitutional authority to manage health services; and (3) delivery of family planning services was restricted by reliance on the facilities of the general health care delivery system.

The first consequence of India's decision to consider family planning a health subject was that it placed the program squarely in the Health Ministry. Medical personnel and health services have an essential role in the provision of most currently available contraceptives; nevertheless, there is no overriding necessity to wholly integrate the policy-making and administrative functions of a family planning program into the same administrative structure responsible for health services. It would be possible to constitute the program as an interministerial authority or to place it in a ministry other than health, such as a social welfare or development-oriented ministry which already possesses greater budgetary and political leverage as well as the capacity to call upon the resources of other governmental agencies. Health ministries in the developing nations are not powerful ministries in the competition for resources within the government. The Health Ministry in India, for example, has never been headed by a person with an independent political base capable of successfully vying for financial, administrative, and political support with ministries and programs considered to be more vital to India's economic growth and development.

The decision to retain the family planning program in the Health Ministry meant that the program was subject to the controls and restraints of the ministry in the exercise of authority and the allocation of resources. Instead of acquiring the status of an independent agency, family planning became, instead, another claimant—and not a strong one, initially—for resources within the Health Ministry in competition with the traditional health services that were more consistent with the values of the medical profession and in greater demand with the client population. Family planning was, in effect, a minor part of a weak ministry headed by doctors whose professional orientation led them to see fertility control as a personal health question rather than a national social objective. John P. Lewis, a careful student of Indian development, has commented on the situation:

It left family planning lodged in what, in the eyes of most observers, remains one of the weakest functional cadres in the Indian administrative system—most hesitant in effecting expeditious bureaucratic clearances, most subservient to the finance ministry overlords who pre-audit its operations—and one in which enervating frictions between administrative (generalists) and technical (medical) personnel already were a long standing tradition.[38]

As the Indian program was granted no extraordinary status, it functioned under the same personnel and finance regulations that applied to all other Indian government agencies. These constraints led to lengthy delays in spending funds, an inability to hire needed personnel, and a generally undermanned professional staff at the national level. Whether the administrative leadership of the program recognized the deficiency or whether they simply could not bend the "steel frame" is conjectural. What is certain is that there was no dramatic variation from the administrative structure that prevailed in most Indian ministries.[39] If the national program had had more high-level personnel with authority to make judgments and decisions on behalf of the ministry, it could have maintained regular and continuous contact with the states and would have been in a position to assist the states with the numerous management and technical problems that arose. Without sufficient high-level personnel, the relationship between the center and the states was intermittent and irregular. In addition to more regular high-level liaison with the states, the central ministry could have maintained closer contact with foreign and international donor agencies and with private and voluntary organizations and associations throughout India who were potentially capable of contributing in some way to India's family planning effort. Some staff were assigned to assume these responsibilities, but they were not of sufficient status or high enough in the system to carry out their responsibilities without referring an inordinate number of questions to their administrative superiors.

The second major consequence of India's decision to declare family planning a health subject was that it became the primary responsibility of the Indian states rather than the central government. The Indian Constitution provides for a federal system and specifies the subjects for which the states are responsible—one of which is health. Consequently, the central government in New Delhi was severely limited in the actions it could independently carry out with regard to family planning on a national level. The central government could not require the states to implement family planning programs, nor could it hire the requisite personnel to work in states that showed little initiative on their own. It could only make funds available, offer to train personnel, and provide guidelines for action; the actual implementation of the program was dependent upon the willingness of the states to act, and the states were not uniformly disposed to accept family planning as a high priority program. Thus the center could appropriate funds, but these appropriations could be underspent by the states; the center could conduct research on contraceptives and make technical recommendations, but the states could ignore these recommendations and utilize any family planning method they preferred; and the center could establish program goals, but the states could carry on their activities largely independent of these goals.

The central government could not circumvent the states in working with the districts. This was a disadvantage to the program, as the districts constituted the critical subunits of government where family planning workers came into direct contact with the target population. The difficulties of providing central guidance were compounded by the subordinate status of the District Family Planning Officer, who, under most state health organizations, was dependent on the staff and facilities controlled by the District Health Officer, a medical doctor.

A third consequence which followed from India's initial decision to declare family planning a health subject was that the program was organized in conjunction with its health care delivery system. Most contraceptive technologies require the services of medical personnel and also require a high and sustained level of motivation on the part of the user. Under these conditions, the Indian family planning program would have been expected to build an organization with a significant "outreach" component—extension agents, field workers, health educators—backed up by a strong communication and information effort. In the early years of the program, however, instead of utilizing outreach techniques or the extension approach, the Indian program depended on a strategy of attracting clients by offering medical and contraceptive services at an expanded number of health clinics serving in a dual capacity as family planning clinics.

In 1963 the government attempted to reorganize the program to "emphasize extension education, greater availability of contraceptive supplies, and less dependence upon the traditional clinical approach."[40] Even after undergoing a modest reorganization, the health delivery system did not demonstrate the initiative or the imagination to formulate an outreach program capable of attracting adopters in sufficient numbers to satisfy the family planning program goals. To be sure, the problem was extraordinarily difficult: the IUD, the pill, and sterilization are not the best technologies for an outreach program. Moreover, the target population was not highly motivated to practice birth control. On the other hand, the health delivery system did not capitalize to any great extent on the potential strength of private organizations or other sources of expertise outside the health system. This program deficiency was underscored in 1965 by two different evaluation reports, one by a United Nations team, and the other by an evaluation group of the Indian Planning Commission.[41] Given a superior contraceptive technology and a population motivated to curtail its fertility, reliance on the existing health care system to administer and implement family planning might have been appropriate. The relatively greater difficulty involved in "selling" family planning in a developing country in contrast to some other health and social programs, however, may point to the need for more commitment, resources, and flexibility if a program aimed at fertility control is to fulfill its objectives.

Pakistan

In the light of subsequent developments, it might be expected that Pakistan's initial efforts in the field of family planning would stand out in sharp contrast to those of India. Actually the earlier years of Pakistan's program paralleled those of India in terms of weak commitment, an inadequate technology, a health-dominated approach, and modest expenditures. Between 1960 and 1964, of almost 25 million rupees committed to family planning programs by Pakistan's Second Five Year Plan, only slightly more than 9 million rupees had been spent.[42] By most conventional measurements, Pakistan's performance in this period was not impressive: acceptance rates were low, clinics were poorly utilized, and the training of new personnel was below expectations.

A series of developments in the program eventually proved crucial, however, in enabling Pakistan's program to achieve a high performance level in subsequent years. Between 1960 and 1964, with the financial support and technical assistance of foreign agencies and universities, Pakistan established a number of centers designed to train family planning personnel, conduct population research, and carry out program evaluation.

The most significant transformation was an outgrowth of Pakistan's thorough involvement and participation in the field testing and evaluation of the IUD. Pakistan's relationship to the worldwide program of the IUD evaluation stands in contrast to India's relative detachment. Pakistan followed up its experimental phase of the program by organizing a large scale "demonstration" to disseminate the new technology. In contrast to India, Pakistan's brief experience with conventional contraceptive technologies prior to the IUD had not induced in the program a pervasive atmosphere of frustration and skepticism. Indicative of the determination and even optimism that began to permeate the program, the Commissioner of Family Planning, Enver Adil, proclaimed that "family planning is essentially [an] administrative and not a clinical program."[43]

Based on the initial favorable reports of the efficacy of the IUD and with the strong support of President Ayub, plans were formulated for the National Family Planning Scheme to commence in July, 1965. During the year preceding the inauguration of the new scheme, expenditures far in excess of all previous family planning funding levels were utilized, and many more personnel were trained and hired to prepare for the major effort. In comparison to India, Pakistan set a relatively modest target for its program. Pakistan's family planning target was aimed at reducing the birth rate from 50 to 40 per 1000 by 1970.[44] The relatively modest target of Pakistan's family planning program constituted a basis for designing a family planning delivery system to reach the number of acceptors necessary to realize the program's goals. In effect, the target was a guideline to the number of medical personnel required for the program, midwives, health clinics, vehicles, and the range of other personnel and equipment essential to an effective delivery system.

In summary, while Pakistan initially had also followed the path of political and administrative convenience, by 1965 it had accomplished a fundamental reorganization of its family planning program. The essential feature of this reorganization was that Pakistan had decided to treat family planning as a top priority program basic to its economic development rather than as a subcategory of health. This decision had several major consequences: (1) Pakistan gave the family planning program autonomy from the Health Ministry; (2) the government established centralized control over important dimensions of the program; and (3) rather than relying entirely on the health structure, it utilized a variety of methods to deliver services. A fuller examination of each of these consequences will reveal more clearly the ways in which Pakistan's family planning program differed from India's.

(1) Pakistan restructured the program as an autonomous entity only nominally within the Ministry of Health, Labour, and Social Welfare. It was then independent for administrative purposes from the health services, and program managers were granted an extraordinary degree of freedom in controlling their own budget and personnel policies. The Family Planning Council was authorized to hire personnel without going through the lengthy procedures to which other agencies were subject and to establish a salary structure higher than that generally applicable to government servants. The employees of the family planning organization were never brought into the conventional government services; they enjoyed the benefits of employment and, for some, a higher level of income, but they also could be more easily dismissed than regular civil servants. The combination was a strong incentive to effective performance.

(2) Instead of being required to respect the constitutional powers of eighteen diverse states, the Central Family Planning Council of Pakistan had to be concerned with only two provinces, both of which were responsive to its direction. Although the provinces had legal authority over the programs, they were, in effect, cooperative instruments of a unified program, not only in accepting policy direction, but also in providing funds.

As was indicated earlier in this paper, however, the provinces differed in their methods and performance. The vasectomy program in East Pakistan achieved substantially greater results than in West Pakistan, although the latter showed relatively greater success with the IUD. The quality of information and data relative to vasectomy adopters is not sufficient to provide a definitive reason for this variation. Based on what is known of the sterilization program in East Pakistan, the answer may not lie with the characteristics of the adopters but may once again be found in the policy and administration of the national program. The national family planning program exerted considerable pressure on the two provinces and their districts to produce results and supported them with funds and other resources in order to attain performance targets. In addition, the Commissioner of Family Planning and other administrators associated with the program at the national level exercised considerable control and guidance to assure the effective implementation of the program.

In West Pakistan, geography and logistics made it possible to carry through with this kind of supervision; in East Pakistan, however, inadequate communications on both technical and cultural levels made it more difficult for the national government to know what was happening in the program and oversee its day-to-day activities. As the IUD program did not progress in East Pakistan as it did in the West, provincial program administrators sought other ways to achieve family planning targets. The pressure from the center for measurable results almost forced them to seek alternatives, and the financial resources enabled them to do so. Freed of the close supervision of the center, East Pakistani family planning officials introduced a financial incentive scheme including inducements to sterilization adopters as well as to private and public officials who performed services in connection with the vasectomy. The use of economic incentives in effect short-circuited much of the energy and resources which would have had to be invested in other methods of motivation. Although the vasectomy poses some difficulties in gaining converts and requires doctors to perform the minor operation, it neither has the adverse side-effects of the IUD nor requires the follow-up procedures entailed by the IUD and other methods. Program officials, however, had only modest expectations for the vasectomy program in Pakistan, and it came as a surprise to them that East Pakistan was achieving significant results—far ahead of schedule—and that sterilization had become an important component of Pakistan's program.

Under President Ayub the Pakistani program introduced a significant degree of decentralization at the district level in order to permit flexibility in responding to local needs, a feature of the program noted and endorsed by the UN evaluation team in 1969.[45] The nominal head of family planning in each district is the deputy commissioner who serves as chairman of the District Family Planning Board. In Pakistan as in India, the deputy commissioner is by far the most powerful administrative position within a district. The deputy commissioner has an authoritative hand in almost every governmental program carried out within his district; he can give high priority to certain programs and ignore others, and he is a member of the nation's most prestigious administrative cadre. His promotion and future depend to a great extent on how his superiors evaluate him in an annual confidential report. As one of the responsibilities assigned to the deputy commissioner is family planning, the director of the national program has the authority to include in a deputy commissioner's annual confidential report an evaluation of his work in carrying out the district family planning program. As a result, the program at the district level was administratively supported as well as led by the deputy commissioner, who assured coordination with other on-going programs in the district. District and lower level officials recognized that Enver Adil, Ayub's commissioner of family planning, functioned under a powerful presidential mandate, which greatly enhanced his influence in the districts. In addition, as a senior member of the civil service of Pakistan, Adil was often dealing with more junior members of the same elite administrative cadre.

Unlike the Indian family planning program, Pakistan's program was able to maintain regular and direct relations with the districts. A management information and feedback system alerted the leadership to problems and deficiencies in program implementation. The national ministry had established a central evaluation unit within each province which performed detailed and technical examinations of each district's family planning program. This procedure permitted the head of the national program to obtain directly from the local level certain types of information significant for policy and managerial purposes. Each province, moreover, maintained a research complex which served as an additional source of information about program activities. The national government also sent an inspection team to visit each district in Pakistan on a quarterly basis. These visits lasted for four or five days at a time and involved an evaluation of the family planning program with attention to the program's relationship to other administrative and developmental programs in the district. Both the evaluation units and the inspection teams were important ways by which Commissioner Adil "kept on top of developments in each district."[46]

(3) Pakistan's program, although once part of the health system, avoided exclusive or primary dependence on the health services while at the same time utilizing the health structure to achieve its goals. No less than the Indian family planning program, the Pakistani program also required the services of medical personnel and health clinics.[47] Rather than integrating the administrative aspects of family planning with health, however, Pakistan vested authority and responsibility for the program in a more dynamic and independent structure.[48] As a result, the program could capitalize on the special resources of the health services by providing them with funds to carry out family planning activities. The program, however, was not exclusively dependent on the health services: it could work out similar financial arrangements with other governmental as well as nongovernmental agencies to perform other functions; it could compensate and utilize private physicians, indigenous midwives, and various para-medical personnel for rendering family planning services; and it could grant monetary rewards on almost a piecework basis to personnel, including those already employed by the government, for their contributions to the program.

The Role of Foreign Assistance

Foreign assistance has been an important component of Indian and Pakistani development programs; compared to India, however, Pakistan has enjoyed a favored status as a recipient of foreign aid, especially from the United States. Between 1966 and 1968, a typical period, Pakistan received $480 million and India received $1191 million in net official receipts (nonmilitary) from bilateral and multilateral donors, making them the two leading recipients in the world.[49] On a per capita basis, however, aid for the same period totalled $3.96 for Pakistan as opposed to $2.32 for India.[50]

Pakistan's favored status was initially a consequence of the country's serious economic plight in the late 1950s when General Ayub assumed power. A large infusion of foreign aid seemed essential to the country's unity and stability. Moreover, Pakistan's domestic and foreign policies under Ayub were congenial to the United States. Unlike India, where government controls and the public sector of the economy were emphasized, Pakistan adopted policies that gave considerable latitude and support to the private sector. Whereas in international relations India adopted a policy of neutrality, Pakistan aligned itself with the U.S. and the West and became an important member of CENTO and SEATO. Later Pakistan strengthened its credentials as a recipient by demonstrating under Ayub a capacity to utilize such assistance effectively. Pakistan, in contrast to India, was highly receptive to the advice of donor nations and showed little of the national sensitivity so much evident in India where foreign advisors and experts were regarded as a necessary form of external interference in Indian affairs.

Foreign aid played a significant role in the Indian and Pakistani population programs by providing financial and technical inputs which had the effect of loosening up domestic resources that might not otherwise have been as readily available for family planning purposes. Foreign aid had this effect, especially in the initial stages of the two programs, because organized efforts at limiting population growth were still largely untried and experimental. As was pointed out earlier, even when family planning programs are successful, the returns are delayed, invisible, and, in the short range, of questionable political value. It is easier for a nation, therefore, to employ foreign funds earmarked for family planning as venture capital and to utilize foreign expertise than to divert scarce domestic resources and personnel from more conventional development projects.

As with foreign aid generally, Pakistan's family planning program was a proportionately greater beneficiary of outside assistance. Despite a population roughly one-fourth the size of India's, Pakistan received $6.8 million from fiscal 1966 through fiscal 1968 for its family planning program compared to $6.3 million for India's, according to figures compiled by Warren Robinson.[51] Pakistan demonstrated early that it was prepared to tackle the population question with a level of energy and determination that was absent in India and was more willing than India to take advantage of the advice and skills of foreign technical advisors. These factors in turn became a justification for the greater interest shown by donor nations in the Pakistan program.

Conclusion

In the period covered by this analysis, Pakistan was more successful than India in pursuing economic development as well as population control, but was the less successful of the two in its political development. If India is susceptible to the accusation that it made too many concessions to politics, Pakistan is even more vulnerable to the opposite accusation that it was not sensitive enough to the needs of the political sector. Guided by the philosophy that economic growth is not only its own reward but is a nation's long-range guarantee of political stability, Pakistan ordered its political life and its policies to maximize its capacity to generate and sustain rapid economic growth. While the private sector was given a free hand, the distribution crisis worsened; while issues of economic location were resolved in an economically "rational" fashion, geographical disparities were intensified; while the classical model of subsidizing urban and industrial development at the expense of the agricultural sector was pursued, peasant dissatisfaction grew; while entrepreneurship was rewarded, the intelligentsia rebelled.[52] These were difficult policy decisions for Ayub and his government, as the outcomes could clearly lead to the loss of vital political support. With the encouragement of both domestic and foreign economic advisors, Ayub nevertheless opted for economics at the expense of politics, a choice which ultimately led to political collapse, a new cycle of military intervention in Pakistan's politics, and civil war.[53]

It is still difficult to ascertain with confidence why the post-Ayub family planning program showed so marked a decline in performance even before the military stage of the conflict between East and West Pakistan. After Ayub, national concerns in Pakistan turned elsewhere, and all development programs slowed down. Even during the last months of the Ayub regime, however, the family planning program became the target of mounting criticism. Seemingly because Ayub had given it his wholehearted support, it became a substitute target for the president. When Ayub himself became the subject of open political criticism there was no need for a substitute target, and the criticism of the family planning program subsided.[54]

A serious liability of the post-Ayub family planning program may have been its distinctive status, semiindependent from the Health Ministry and exempt from the conventional civil service and financial regulations. These measures of autonomy were designed to give the program the freedom and flexibility to hire and spend in order to achieve program objectives, but without Ayub in power to assure the continuation of the distinct status of the program, it was an organization in limbo without moorings in the established bureaucratic structure of the country. Its workers who had been hired under extraordinary regulations were no longer protected; it could not depend upon the support of the Health Ministry to carry out its activities; and it remained an anathema to an administrative system which still adhered to much more conventional rules and regulations. The advantage of autonomy under Ayub may therefore have produced more serious disadvantages to the family planning program after his political demise than if it had been a program which had been upgraded in the conventional structure rather than being made separate from it.

In contrast to Pakistan, India has shown considerable commitment to Western parliamentary government as well as ideological dedication to socialism and egalitarianism. Much more indigenous to India has been its commitment to conciliation and bargaining as a means of resolving internal conflict. These characteristics are reflected in the country's competitive party system, the absence of military intervention in politics, the continuation of a free press, the constitutional as well as *de facto* strength of the states, and a range of significant as well as symbolic policies adopted by the government in every area of social life. While India has not been economically stagnant, at no time has India shown the political capacity or the will to go all-out for rapid economic growth, especially if such growth would necessitate major compromises for the political system. India's performance in family planning remains roughly comparable to its performance in other program areas, but the continuity of the program, the comparatively stable political environment, and the accumulation of knowledge and experience in running the program may at least constitute a basis for more impressive results in the future.

The experience and relative performance of India and Pakistan in administering national family planning programs are functionally related to each nation's politics and development strategy. Considerable evidence has been presented in this chapter indicating that the properties of a nation's political system and its development policies are important determinants of program performance.[55] Paradoxically, the strength of Pakistan's family planning program is closely associated with factors that have spelled disruption and breakdown for Pakistan's political development. The comparative weakness of India's effort to control population growth is linked to the viability of its democratic political institutions as well as to its less impressive performance in achieving more rapid economic growth during the 1960s.

Notes

1. George B. Simmons, *The Indian Investment in Family Planning* (New York: Occasional Paper of the Population Council, 1971), p. 181. Earlier predictions of U.S. demographers had also underestimated the degree of population growth. See Ansley Coale and Edgar M. Hoover, *Population Growth and Eco-*

nomic Development in Low-Income Countries (Princeton, N.J.: Princeton University Press, 1958).

2. Lee L. Bean, "Pakistan's Population in the 1970's: Certainties and Uncertainties" (Paper delivered at annual meeting of the Association for Asian Studies, Washington, D.C., March 30, 1971); and J. Gilbert Hardee and Adaline P. Satterthwaite, "Pakistan," *Country Profiles* (New York: The Population Council, March, 1970), pp. 1-2.

3. John P. Lewis, "Population Control in India," *Population Bulletin* 26, no. 5 (November, 1970): 15-16. Although Lewis presents evidence limited to India, his information on this point is equally applicable to Pakistan.

4. Marshall Balfour, "Chairman's Report of a Panel Discussion on Comparative Acceptability of Different Methods of Contraception," in Clyde V. Kiser (ed.), *Research in Family Planning* (Princeton, N.J.: Princeton University Press, 1962), pp. 373-86.

5. India had supplemented the conventional array of mechanical and chemical contraceptives by making available in some areas both male and female sterilization. Neither country offered the pill through its government-sponsored program because of concern over cost, side-effects, and the belief that the regimen of the one-a-day pill would not be followed by most women.

6. S.J. Segal, A.L. Southern, and K.D. Shafer (eds.), *Intra-Uterine Contraception: Proceedings of the Second International Conference, New York City, 2-3 October, 1964* (Amsterdam: Excerpta Medica International Congress Series No. 86).

7. In 1969 when a team of experts from a United Nations evaluation mission reviewed the Indian family planning program, they indicated that "the optimistic view of the IUD generally prevailing at that time was largely responsible for their [subsequent problems] not having been fully appreciated. Lack of an effective evaluation mechanism in the programme for promptly analyzing such problems aggravated the difficulties." United Nations, Secretariat, U.N. Advisory Mission, *An Evaluation of the Family Planning Programme of the Government of India* (ST/SOA/SER.R/11), November 24, 1969, p. 6.

8. Albert O. Hirschman, *Development Projects Observed* (Washington, D.C.: The Brookings Institution, 1967), p. 13.

9. The literature of social demography is replete with discussions of the social correlates of fertility. See, for example, Dudley Kirk, "A New Demographic Transition," in National Academy of Sciences Study Committee, *Rapid Population Growth* (Baltimore: The Johns Hopkins Press, 1971), pp. 123-47. Comparative data on India and Pakistan are assembled in Dorothy Nortman, "Population and Family Planning Programs: A Factbook," *Reports on Population/ Family Planning*, no. 2 (New York: The Population Council, 1971).

10. Bernard Berelson, "National Family Planning Programs: Where We Stand," in S.J. Behrman, Leslie Corsa, Jr., and Ronald Freedman (eds.), *Fertility and Family Planning: A World View* (Ann Arbor: University of Michigan Press, 1969), p. 375.

11. For example, see Byung Moo Lee and John Isbister, "The Impact of Birth Control Programs on Fertility," in Bernard Berelson et al. (eds.), *Family Planning and Population Programs* (Chicago: The University of Chicago Press, 1966), pp. 737-58; Robert G. Potter, Jr., "Estimating Births Averted in a Family Planning Program," in Behrman, Corsa, and Freedman (n. 10), pp. 413-34; D. Wolfers, "The Demographic Effects of a Contraceptive Programme," *Population Studies* 23, no. 1 (March 1969): 111-40; Simmons (n. 1), pp. 41-76; and K. Venkatacharya, "A Model to Estimate Births Averted Due to IUCD's and Sterilizations," *Demography* 8, no. 4 (November, 1971): 491-505; Jack Reynolds, "Evaluation of Family Planning Program Performance," *Demography* 9, no. 1 (February, 1972): 69-86.

12. Berelson (n. 10), p. 373; Potter (n. 11), p. 432.

13. Wajihuddin Ahmad, "Field Structures in Family Planning," *Studies in Family Planning* 2, no. 1 (January, 1971), p. 7. These remarks by the Commissioner of Family Planning were published after the resignation of President Ayub Khan and are probably more openly critical of the earlier program administration than would normally be expected.

14. Lewis (n. 3), pp. 16-17.

15. Reports of several studies on age, parity, or IUD retention of family planning adopters in India and Pakistan have appeared in *Studies in Family Planning* (New York: The Population Council, 1963-1970). See issue nos. 1, 8, 18, 31, 35, 39, 47, and 56. The judgment attributed to "first hand observers" is based on numerous discussions the author has had with representatives and experts from U.S. and international agencies and universities.

16. Department of Family Planning, *Progress of Family Planning Programme in India* (New Delhi: Government of India, 1970).

17. With the exception of 1967, OECD/DAC figures show Pakistan several percentage points higher than India in its annual GDP growth rate from 1960-69. Organisation for Economic Co-operation and Development, *1971 Review: Development Assistance—Efforts and Policies of Members of the Development Assistance Committee* (Paris: OECD Publications, 1971), p. 199. According to Mason, in the 1950s Pakistan's performance was "miserable," and India showed a comparative advantage in economic growth. In his study he devotes much attention to explaining the reasons for the "striking reversal" which occurred in the first half of the 1960s. Edward S. Mason, *Economic Development in India and Pakistan*, Harvard University Center for International Affairs Occasional Papers in International Affairs, no. 13 (Cambridge, Mass., 1966).

18. A.H. Hanson, "Power Shifts and Regional Balances," in Paul Streeten and Michael Lipton (eds.), *The Crisis in Indian Planning: Economic Policy in the 1960's* (London: Oxford University Press, 1968), p. 26.

19. Khalid B. Sayeed, *The Political System of Pakistan* (Boston: Houghton Mifflin Company, 1967), p. 102.

20. As quoted in Lucian W. Pye, "Party Systems and National Development

in Asia," in Joseph LaPalombara and Myron Weiner (eds.), *Political Parties and Political Development* (Princeton, N.J.: Princeton University Press, 1966), p. 369.

21. Gustav Papanek, *Pakistan's Development: Social Goals and Private Incentives* (Cambridge, Mass.: Harvard University Press, 1967), p. 6.

22. Lipset states that "prolonged effectiveness over a number of generations may give legitimacy to a political system. In the modern world, such effectiveness means primarily constant economic development." Seymour M. Lipset, *Political Man: The Social Bases of Politics* (New York: Doubleday and Company, Inc., 1960), p. 82. For an interesting discussion of this question, see Warren F. Ilchman and Norman Thomas Uphoff, *The Political Economy of Change* (Berkeley: University of California Press, 1969), especially pp. 111-114.

23. Papanek (n. 21), p. 6.

24. Mahbub-ul-Haq, "Pakistan's Economic Choices for the 1970's" (Paper delivered at the annual meeting of the Association for Asian Studies, Washington, D.C., March 30, 1971), p. 2.

25. Ibid.

26. For further analysis of Pakistan's approach to economic development and the role of the private sector, see a critical and perceptive article by Timothy and Leslie Nulty, "Pakistan: The Busy Bee Route to Development," *Transaction* 8, no. 4 (February 1971): 18-26ff.

27. Merle Fainsod, "The Structure of Development Administration," in Irving Swerdlow (ed.), *Development Administration: Concepts and Problems* (Syracuse: Syracuse University Press, 1963), p. 14.

28. Albert Waterston, *Planning in Pakistan: Organization and Implementation* (Baltimore, Md.: The Johns Hopkins Press, 1963), p. 77; and Papanek (n. 21), p. 85.

29. Hanson (n. 18), p. 55.

30. Mason (n. 17), pp. 6-7.

31. Address to Food Conference in Lahore, January, 1959. Indian leaders have often made similar pronouncements, but, in my judgment, Ayub was strongly committed to this position, as his subsequent behavior indicated.

32. Dr. Shamin A. Jafarey, former Deputy Commissioner of Family Planning in Pakistan, interview in Ann Arbor, Michigan, April 17, 1969.

33. Simmons (n. 1), p. 183, concludes that despite the emphasis given to population control in written statements emanating from the Indian Planning Commission, the Commission actually attached low salience to population. He advances two fundamental reasons for the discrepancy between words and action: "First, although per capita income has been indicated to be the major goal of Indian economic planning, it seems likely that the major operational goal is total national income. Second, the early plans were based on demographic and economic models which did not leave any role for population policy." These findings suggest additional reasons why Indian planning might have been more

easily diverted from population control as a result of political considerations.

34. Shri Govind Narain, Secretary to the Ministry of Health, Family Planning
and Urban Development, "India: The Family Planning Program Since 1965,"
Studies in Family Planning, no. 35 (November, 1968), p. 2.

35. Nicholas J. Demerath, "Can India Reduce its Birth Rate? A Question of
Modernization and Organizational Capacity," *The Journal of Social Issues* 3, no.
4 (October, 1967): 179-94.

36. Narain (n. 34), p. 2.

37. See, for example, B.L. Raina, *Family Planning Programme Report for
1962-63* (New Delhi: Directorate General of Health Services, Ministry of Health,
Government of India, 1964).

38. Lewis (n. 3), p. 18.

39. In his analysis of Indian public administration, Paul Appleby elaborated
on the stifling effect of the system's bureaucratic controls. *Re-examination of
India's Administrative System* (New Delhi: Government of India, Cabinet Secretariat, 1956).

40. Demerath (n. 35), p. 184.

41. United Nations, Department of Economic and Social Affairs, *Report on
the Family Planning Programme of India* (TAO/IND/48), 1966; and Programme
Evaluation Organisation, Planning Commission, Government of India, *Evaluation
of the Family Planning Programme* (1965).

42. Enver Adil, "Pakistan," in Berelson et al. (n. 11), p. 127.

43. Ministry of Health, Government of Pakistan, *Family Planning Scheme for
Pakistan* (1965).

44. Enver Adil, "Pakistan: The Family Planning Program, 1965-1967,"
Studies in Family Planning, no. 26 (New York: The Population Council, 1968),
p. 4.

45. United Nations/World Health Organization Advisory Mission, Secretariat,
United Nations, *Report on an Evaluation of the Family Planning Programme of
the Government of Pakistan* (ST/SOA/SER.R/9), April 7, 1969, p. 22.

46. Personal interview with Dr. Nafis Sadik, Director General of the Pakistan
Family Planning Council, Ann Arbor, Michigan, May 18, 1971.

47. The UN/WHO evaluation report on Pakistan (n. 45), p. 43, pointed out
that the framework of the health services "reached only about 10% of the rural
population." The Report also suggested that the underdeveloped health services
of Pakistan were one of the factors which induced the government to establish a
separate family planning organization.

48. Although the thesis presented here attributes much of the success of
Pakistan's program to administrative separation from the health services, the
combined United Nations/World Health Organization, evaluation mission was
somewhat critical of this separation (n. 45), pp. 47-50. The position of the
UN/WHO mission reflects a consistent view of WHO in favor of treating family
planning as an integral aspect of health.

49. Organisation for Economic Co-operation and Development, *1969 Review: Development Assistance—Efforts and Policies of Members of the Development Assistance Committee* (Paris: OECD Publications, 1970), p. 318.

50. Ibid.

51. Warren Robinson, "A Cost-effectiveness Analysis of Selected National Family Planning Programs," mimeographed (University Park, Pa.: Pennsylvania State University, 1969).

52. Nulty (n. 26).

53. At the outset of his study on the role of the military, Janowitz observes: "Those organizational and professional qualities which make it possible for the military of a new nation to accumulate political power, and even to take over political power, are the same as those which limit its ability to rule effectively." Morris Janowitz, *The Military in the Political Development of New Nations* (Chicago: The University of Chicago Press, 1964), p. 1.

54. AID reported that criticism in Pakistan of the Ayub regime was related to the decline in program performance. Office of Population, Bureau for Technical Assistance, Agency for International Development, *Population Program Assistance* (Washington, D.C., October, 1970), p. 163.

55. The combination of politics and development strategy that may seem highly productive for one field of development, however, may not be functional for another field. For example, in contrast with family planning, consider the impact of these factors on community development, where India has been more successful than Pakistan. See, for example, A.T.R. Rahman, "Theories of Administrative and Political Development and Rural Institutions in India and Pakistan" Southeast Asia Development Advisory Group Papers on Development and Development Policy Problems, No. 23 (1967).

7 Political Philosophy and Population Policy: Insights and Blindspots of a Tradition

Lewis Lipsitz

—Our guardians, then, I said, will find here the fairest standard by which to regulate the size of the city. They may then set apart land in proportion, and let the rest alone.

—What standard? he asked

—This, in my opinion, I said, The city may go on increasing so long as it can grow without losing its unity, but no further.

—Yes, that is excellent, he said

—Then we shall lay this further command upon the guardians, that they take every precaution that the city be neither small nor of illusory greatness, but of sufficient size and unity.

—Well, that is certainly a trifling task, he said.

—Here is another, I said, still more trifling . . . . The other citizens as well as the guardians must be set each to the task for which nature has fitted him, one man one task, that so each citizen doing his own particular work may become one man and not many, and thus the whole city may grow to be not many cities, but one.

—Yes, he said, that is a smaller affair than the former.

Book IV, *The Republic*

We can see in this trifling Platonic discussion some of the concerns with population that recur in the tradition of Western political thought. Most important, we see that from Plato and Aristotle among the ancients, to Machiavelli, Rousseau and various utopians among the more moderns—population *matters*. It matters how many people there are, how they are distributed, in what ways they are organized, how rapidly they are increasing, and what sort of training they receive. In the quote above, Plato is obviously interested in the issue of size, although he is more fundamentally concerned with the problem of unity. It is this principle of unity, or each in his proper role, that shapes his attitude toward population. A unified city would be a city without frictions which could therefore function more justly and effectively than cities torn by internal divisions, such as those between the rich and the poor. Immediately then, we see a concern with population size tied to other concerns, and most notably to the issues of internal stability and the quality of rule.

Plato's *Republic*, of course, is a utopian document, in the sense that it seeks to set out the guiding principles for the creation of a good polity—one that will have to be insulated from corrupting changes that arise both internally and externally.[1] Aristotle, in his discussion of the "best" state, is also concerned about population size. He argues that two principles should govern in this area: first, that the population should be large enough to be able to provide for economic self-sufficiency; second, that the population be small enough so that the citizens can acquire knowledge of each other's characters.[2] In other words: that one need not depend on taxi drivers for one's sense of what is happening in the polity. There is in Aristotle's discussion, as in Plato's, the sense that too large a population will lose its identity as a single political entity and this will therefore lead to problems of "law and order."

This preference for homogeneity and self-sufficiency persists in Rousseau and Machiavelli. In the latter, as in Plato, population size is significant in part because of the need to be able to counter external threats. The realities of international conflict shape a portion of the argument. Machiavelli argues, for example, that in measuring the strength of a state the main factor to take account of is whether it can maintain itself in war without help of another state. This is not *just* a matter of population, but it includes the availability of manpower.[3] From both a "utopian" or "ideal" point of view and one of international "realism," then, the issue of population cannot be ignored.

As we can see already, however, the context of classical discussions was radically different from our own contemporary situation, although there are strong similarities. The ancients were concerned with a situation of relative rather than of absolute overpopulation. They saw the problem of the polity expanding beyond a healthy size, but this was not for them a global problem whose dimensions could not be escaped. In fact, it was precisely Plato's idea that establishing a new and more unified polity would allow an escape from the conflicts present elsewhere. It was also impossible for these writers to take industrial technology into account. Such technology changes the dimensions of the problem by allowing wider communication and increased economic productivity. Yet the basic issues of economic viability and of a knowledgeable citizenry, as posed by Aristotle, remain, however altered the form of the tensions. The classical concern for population as related to the good life also remains. In Plato and Aristotle, the quality of life is determined primarily by factors other than population size, distribution, and degree of homogeneity; but these factors are not ignored.

What the ancients could not consider was the very idea of economic development itself—the notion that the fundamental economic base on which political viability would be built might itself be altered to allow for support of a considerably larger population. Nor, of course, could they therefore weigh the various conflicts and problems of the development process and how these might be related to questions of population. These issues, so significant for "development" theory, will be considered later.

It should also be noted here that the spectre of war appears right from the beginnings of political philosophy as part of the discussion of population. Again, the context of such discussion must now be different. We are now in the odd position of being able to ponder our own extermination and not just the defeat of our city. The range of destructive possibilities is now much greater, yet the element of power that previous theorists perceived in population questions is still with us.

Liberalism, Marxism, and Population

For most "modern" thinkers, at least until very recently, the classical perspectives on population seemed startlingly alien. In the liberal and Marxist traditions, most writers have in common the fact that they turn away from such discussions and, equipped with a profound technological and psychological optimism, look forward to making the world safe for plenty of everything. John Locke's ideals of nonpaternalism, toleration, life, liberty, and the pursuit of property have no place for worries about too much plenty and too many people. For Locke, there was always a wilderness to be the site for a new state of nature and a new original contract. The early liberal tradition in America, however, has within it many of the "classical" strains. We can see this in the Jeffersonian concern with urbanity as an acid dissolving political civility. The distrust of urban life, however misplaced in some ways, runs counter to the benign optimism implicit in the association of growth with human progress.

Marxism, perhaps even more than liberalism, discounted the problems of development, abundance, and population. Marx's fundamental position was that the human species had sought, fairly successfully, to dominate nature but that in so doing had created forms of social organization which in turn came to dominate the potentialities of the species. Seeking to turn nature to his ends, man created the division of labor, the unforeseen consequences of which shaped his very spirit. This bitter irony—trading domination *of* nature for domination *by* social organization—reaches its sharpest contradiction in capitalism. A socialist form of social organization, Engels argued, would reverse this inherent contradiction and allow man to make his own history, presumably as successfully as he has been able to dominate nature. The species would leave the "realm of necessity" and enter the "realm of freedom."[4]

This Marxist vision, while noble and deep, fails even to cast a glance in the direction of some of the most pressing contemporary problems. Marx not only misunderstood in part the nature of freedom in personal and social life, he also did not think of the negative and problematical consequences of abundance under *any* system of social organization. Or, in any case, he believed such consequences could in turn be resolved by appropriate changes in social organization and control. In this, he may turn out to be largely correct, but in his estimate of the future, there is no trace of the justifiable pessimism, sometimes reaching to apocalyptic proportions, which afflicts many modern analysts. Certainly, he has nothing to tell us about the problems of population since, within his vision they either did not exist, or they resulted only from the forms of organization in nonsocialist societies. We will see later, however, that a different strand of the Marxist tradition, that which focussed on work life, does lead us to take an interest in population issues.

Marx formulated his most touching picture of life in the future Communist society in one of his early writings, *The German Ideology*. His vision went like this:

In communist society, where nobody has one exclusive sphere of activity but each can become accomplished in any branch he wishes, society regulates the general production and thus makes it possible for me to do one thing today and another tomorrow, to hunt in the morning, fish in the afternoon, rear cattle in the evening, criticize after dinner, just as I have a mind, without ever becoming hunter, fisherman, shepherd, or critic.[5]

The division of labor is surmounted. Yet, as Michael Walzer has recently pointed out, the socialist citizen of such a utopian republic, would also want to participate avidly in public debate about the day-to-day as well as the epoch-making decisions in his society. It might go this way:

Before hunting in the morning, this unalienated man of the future is likely to attend a meeting of the Council on Animal Life, where he will be required to vote on important matters relating to the stocking of the forests. The meeting will probably not end much before noon, for among the many-sided citizens there will always be a lively interest even in highly technical problems. Immediately after lunch, a special session of the Fishermen's Council will be called to protest the maximum catch recently voted by the Regional Planning Commission. And the Marxist man will participate eagerly in these debates, even postponing a scheduled discussion of some contradictory theses on cattle-rearing. Indeed, he will probably love argument far better than hunting, fishing, *or* rearing cattle. The debates will go on so long that the citizens will have to rush through dinner in order to assume their role as critics. . . . . Socialism, Oscar Wilde once wrote, would take too many evenings.[6]

Walzer's telling and delightful commentary on Marx's vision omits, however, further complications. For one, the participant citizen would not likely live in a rural but rather in an urban utopia. To reach the Council of Animal Life Meeting he might have to drive uptown on the new highway still under construction and filled with bottlenecks. Rushing to the east side of town for the fishermen's meeting he might find himself held up by an electrical power failure that stopped elevators in that area. By evening, such a many-sided, participant citizen might well be ready to pull his utopian hair out.

As both liberals and Marxists are just beginning to discover, there is no neat one-to-one correspondence between affluence and the quality of existence.

Many old questions need to be reopened and cannot be brushed aside by predictions of further progress. Political philosophers need to reexamine the relationships between population growth, population distribution, and political and personal health. Those who had placed their hopes in industrialization may still do so, but these will have to be somewhat chastened or more circumspect hopes. Moreover, it may become necessary, as I will discuss elsewhere, to look carefully at the issues involved in regulating population growth and the paternalistic implications of such regulation.

While liberal and Marxist visions of the good life and the good state do not lose their significance because of a failure to attend to population issues, it is important to recognize this blindspot of our heritage.

Liberalism and Coercion

Population problems provide us with an interesting and complex focus on liberal theory and the issue of coercion. Liberal theory traditionally has regarded the state as the primary source of coercive power. Following from this perception, "liberals" have feared state action, and the doctrine of laissez faire tries to argue for the inefficiency and coercive nature of governmental as compared with private activities. Taking the self-regulating market as their model, liberals viewed "private" contractual relationships as noncoercive and governmental involvement as a form of force. We have inherited this deep skepticism about state action, and the classical liberal theory continues to crop up in our political life.

As most know now, and as some knew then, liberalism in its earlier forms fails to take adequate account of the "coercions" which arise from nongovernmental sources. While John Stuart Mill could define liberty as doing what one wants—so long as it does not interfere with another's right to do the same—his definition was likely to have very little meaning to the person whose choices were starvation or theft.[7] Such a definition of liberty leaves out of account the issue of the inner capacity for choice as well as the external situation in which one has some "meaningful" alternatives. Without these two elements, "doing what one wants" can be a hollow freedom indeed. Mill was partly aware of such problems, and he does allow room for education's role and also for *some* paternalistic action on the part of the state. Yet, we must now go further.

A more contemporary definition of freedom would have to include explicitly some discussion of both the inner life and of social structure.[8] The notion of coercion would itself have to be considerably broadened and made more subtle and complex. If we look at the population issue in this light we can see the sorts of implications it would hold for liberal theory. First, we would have to consider the various sorts of "coercions," including social pressure, religious training, and so on which induce people to have families of a certain size. Second, we would have to take into account the role of ignorance in determining childbearing.

Third, we would have to look to the social consequences of these social pressures or of ignorance. Finally, even in the case of most people making "free" choices about the sizes of their families, we would have to attend to the society-wide results of these various choices and might have to judge them negatively. If that were so, the "state"—here representing a majority or the collective judgment—might choose to provide incentives for either larger or smaller families.

We can now easily see what the earlier liberals could not: that ignorance and psychological pressures can be as "coercive" as state power; that individual free choices may have disastrous general consequences; and finally that sensible paternalistic policies can increase the net amount of freedom in a society as well as the net amount of well-being. Where the population issue is concerned, the argument for paternalistic legislation seems to me rather strong.[9] First, we are dealing with an area which is often at the center of people's passions and therefore may be difficult for them to control without assistance. Second, it is an area where people often regret later what they have done earlier. Third, it is an area where ignorance abounds. Finally, it is an area of general social consequence.

This does not tell us, of course, what sort of legislation is in order. But within the context of a paternalistic liberalism it would be possible to justify policies ranging from voluntary education at the minimum to compulsory schooling, financial incentives, and even various sorts of penalties, although these last are the most difficult to justify both politically and morally. In more affluent societies where the main issues are not perhaps overall population growth but the excessively large families of some, coupled with maldistribution of the population and large numbers of unwanted children, minimal paternalism would seem to be called for. It is relatively easy to imagine the sorts of educational campaigns, free clinics, and financial incentives that might be tried as ways of redistributing population, reducing the size of some families, and making sure fewer unwanted children were born. If such minimal methods failed, then one might begin thinking about more restrictive prohibitions. But here the high social costs of enforcing such punitive legislation would have to be weighed against the costs of allowing unregulated reproduction.

In the poorer states, the population problem grows far more complicated. In some cases, the issue of absolute size is crucial. In others, the rate of growth must be curtailed, although absolute size has not yet become a problem. In yet others, one or another of these matters may be combined with excessive concentrations of population and excessively rapid migrations. Some of these problems may be amenable to the minimal paternalist styles of policy. Others are probably not going to yield to such partial incentives. In countries like India or Pakistan, even a massive and continuing commitment to investments in family planning may not yield enough results. In such cases the alternatives are bleak. It is clear that where there is a commitment to more-or-less nonauthorization politics, as in India, the sustaining of such a commitment is tied to a certain undetermined rate of social and economic progress. The rate of population increase may thwart such progress and thereby endanger not only economic growth but the unity of the "polis," which may not be all that unified to begin with. A bitter irony, then, could involve relatively nonauthoritarian governments imposing strict population controls to help preserve their nonauthoritarianism. At this point, it seems natural to raise questions about the nature of development itself and whether the way we conceive of it affects the way we conceptualize the problems of population.

Political Theory, Development, and Population

In some sense, much in the tradition of Western political philosophy has been concerned with problems of development. The issues of institution building, equitable rule, sensible resource distribution, sovereignty; and political community occur repeatedly in this tradition. But they do not occur in the context of the possibilities that modern men unavoidably must face. It is no longer possible to regard the economic or social situation as a given. One cannot, with Machiavelli, regard as fixed the basic materials of the state, including the social structure and habits of life of the people. The notion of development now includes the possibility of change even in these "fundamentals." Such a notion implies a kind of Platonic utopianism gone wild.

Precisely this all-encompassing quality of "development" cannot be avoided in our day. The Russian and Chinese Revolutions and other forms of rapid social change—whether directed or undirected—have made it clear that social life can be altered drastically and relatively quickly. For some, this very idea—rapid and drastic change—has become synonymous with development. Development means the abandoning, probably under compulsions of one kind or another, of traditional styles of life and traditional values, and the mobilization of populations in order to take on modern characteristics. Robert Heilbroner has championed this idea with considerable skill, maintaining that in today's poor countries only a revolutionary pace of change can wrench populations out of their traditional lethargy and get the development process in motion. Heilbroner is rather pessimistic, therefore, about development and any sort of "democracy" fitting together in the foreseeable future.[10] Others, of course, take a more moderate view, seeing development as a more gradual process which can incorporate or even seek to sustain certain features of traditional life.

Regardless of how one views the nature of "development," however, one must still deal with the relations between richer and poorer nations. Is the essential problem of the poor nations overpopulation, or is it underdevelopment? Can the problems of the international distribution of wealth be at least partly solved within the framework of capitalism, or is this impossible? Do Western proposals for family planning in the poor countries amount to a new form of Yankee imperialism?[11] These issues are important not only because of the intrinsic merits of the questions themselves but also because they are salient in the minds of intellectuals and politicians in the poorer nations.

There is an international distribution of wealth and, in effect, an international class structure. The population problem, although it aggravates existing inequalities, is not identical with them. Current arguments about "the population bomb," however, emphasize how urgent the population issue is and how it needs immediate attention *quite apart* from remedies for underdevelopment. Clearly, the issue of overpopulation versus underdevelopment varies from one country to another. In all cases, overpopulation makes matters more difficult, but sometimes it is not so simple a matter to define exactly what overpopulation means. Elsewhere, as in India and Pakistan, it is clear that population increases vitiate developmental progress and thereby compounds the problems of change. It ought to be possible for social scientists interested in population and development to establish some criteria for weighting the urgency of development problems versus population problems in various poorer nations. This would provide a guide both for elites in those societies as well as for those who would assist them.

Nonetheless, the issue remains of "exploitative" relations between the richer Western societies and various poor countries. Although the age of traditional colonialism is almost dead, new forms of oppression, or perhaps more significant, of indifference have taken its place. Apparently as a function of "normal" growth, the gap between rich and poor widens. The wealthier countries also find that they can trade more successfully among themselves than with their poorer brethren. Capitalist economies, rather than being indissolubly tied to exploitation of the poorer areas, have become more independent and efficient in the last twenty-five years than ever before. There is no prospect of these successes coming to any disastrous finale in the near future.[12] Since this is the case, the real problems that "wealth" presents are two. First, the insulated rich are likely to become more indifferent to the plight of their distant neighbors because their own wealth is not dependent on developments among the poor. And second, the waste and "over-consumption" characteristic of contemporary capitalist economies leaves a great deal to be desired as a model of development for the poor nations. Though I have been attending mostly to the industrialized west, I want to make it clear that similar strictures apply to the industrialized east. Though Russian industrial development has often been chosen as an appropriate model for the now-developing nations, it is clearly inappropriate if one values the retention of some features of traditional culture and a process of *gradual* as opposed to breath-taking social change.

Some of the leading political figures in the developing nations, as in certain African countries, realize that neither Western nor Soviet models are appropriate for them. This seems to me a decisive step forward. In the literature of political science, the "civic culture" model of Western development is often upheld as the only appropriate form of sociopolitical life. Ironically, once this model is abandoned as out-of-reach of the developing nations, political scientists are frequently ready to advocate many forms of authoritarian rule as somehow appropriate or reasonable at least for the time being. A more sensible position should lie somewhere between these two poles of self-congratulation and cynicism. The "civic culture" may not be an altogether good model, but some features of it may be realizable in many situations. It should not be a question of Western parliamentarianism or military rule. Between these alternatives there are the issues of due process, censorship, limited political competition, independent trade unions, and so on. Likewise, in terms of economic and social development, the alternatives are not industrialization or nothing, or again, capitalism versus socialism. It is time for political scientists to work out various models of development, models which not only aim at different mixes of goals, but also involve different sequences of change, and different rates of change.[13]

In any such discussion, the population variable will be crucial. This is the way in which the population issue can be most sensibly joined to discussions of development, political authority, and the international distribution of wealth. One more word, however, needs to be added here. Though it should go without saying, still one cannot repeat too often that the creation and maintenance of the equipment of violence in both richer and poorer societies is one of the primary drags not only on economic development but on the reasonable evolution of our species. Competition of a more constructive sort, perhaps in the form of nonmilitary assistance to the poorer nations, needs more and more to take its place. Until it does, all our hopes are in jeopardy.

Conclusions: The Political Problem?

In chapter 1 of this book, Lyle Saunders defines seven broad "demogenic" phenomena: rapid population growth; population size; dependency ratios; uneven distribution; the precarious balance between food production and population growth; the dampening effects of population problems on developmental progress; and the environmental implications of population growth, population concentration, and rapid urbanization. It is clear from some of the other papers presented here that the exact definition of what is "demogenic" in a particular case awaits further work. Nonetheless, Saunders' listing provides a starting point for those of us interested in discussing the good polity and various models of development.

If nothing else, the listing makes clear how far we are from the sorts of population concerns one finds in the tradition of Western political thought. In this sense, we are normatively on our own, having to chart out new guidelines of what matters and what is reasonable to suit this radically open-ended situation. From a normative standpoint, we have barely even begun to explore the implications of population problems for political authority and personal freedom. We have also not yet established normative or empirical priorities in terms of research problems and of resolving issues in the "real world."

As we have seen, our tradition has tended to steer us wrong in the case of population problems. This fact leaves the theorist for the moment in an eclectic position where he must grasp at whatever insights and questions seem most promising. It will be part of the work of such a theorist to help us decide what actually *is* a problem, what actually *is* "demogenic." When we talk of urban blight and overconcentration of population we have implicitly in mind some normative standard for judging what better life might be possible. When we insist on people curtailing their birthrate, we have implicitly in mind some way of judging the various "coercions" of a planned versus an unplanned life in regard to population. It is exactly these normative matters—of priorities, relative weights, alternative choices and their costs—that need now to be spelled out. In doing so, we can call on our tradition not perhaps for specific insights, but certainly for the idea that such an enterprise is itself worthwhile and possible.

We can also find in this tradition the idea that we have to maintain some critical distance in dealing with ourselves. Population questions can too easily become the domain in which the relatively affluent preach to the poor—a dubious way of doing business. The affluent also have to see the weaknesses and contradictions of their own societies. "Development," after all, does not cease when incomes reach $1,000 per capita. Exactly here, liberalism and Marxism have a great deal still to teach us and still to learn! From the former, we must learn to redefine liberty in terms more appropriate to industrialized societies. And from the latter, we can acquire an interest in the meaning of community— an idea which has direct implications for population distribution, size, and means of participation. Worker's control, the size of industrial establishments— these issues are among the heritages of Marxism for the discontented affluent. Yet, of course, these matters are also applicable to the poorer countries with proper modifications.

These are certainly "trifling" tasks, Socrates.

Notes

1. For a discussion of Plato's ideas about political stability see Alvin Gouldner, *Enter Plato* (New York: Basic Books, 1965).

2. *The Politics*, book VII, part II.

3. *The Prince*, section X.

4. These phrases are from Engels' work, "Socialism: Utopian and Scientific," in L. Feuer (ed.), *Marx and Engels: Writings on Politics and Philosophy* (New York: Doubleday, 1959).

5. "The German Ideology," in L. Feuer (ed.), *Marx and Engels: Writings on Politics and Philosophy* (New York: Doubleday, 1959).

6. "A Day in the Life of a Socialist Citizen," *Dissent* (May-June 1968), p. 243.

7. See Mill's famous essay *On Liberty*, and for a discussion of these issues, see C. Friedrich (ed.), *Nomos*, vol. 4: *Liberty*, (New York: Atherton, 1962).

8. An interesting beginning to such a discussion is Christian Bay's *The Structure of Freedom* (Stanford, Calif.: Stanford University Press, 1959).

9. See Heilbroner's article, "Counter-Revolutionary America?", *Commentary* (April 1967), pp. 31-38.

10. See Heilbroner's *The Great Ascent* (New York: Harper and Row, 1963).

11. For a discussion of these issues from a new left perspective, see David Eakins, "Population and the Capitalism Bomb: A Review of Paul Ehrlich's *The Population Bomb, Socialist Revolution* (March-April 1970), pp. 144-152.

12. For two discussions see Andrew Shonfield's, *Modern Capitalism* (London: Oxford, 1969), and the debate on imperialism involving Harry Magdoff and S.M. Miller, et. al., in *Social Policy* (September-October 1970), pp. 12-29.

13. Two beginnings along these lines are: William McCord, *The Springtime of Freedom* (New York: Oxford, 1965), and Robert Heilbroner's collection of essays, *Between Capitalism and Socialism* (New York: Vintage, 1970).

8 Political Science in Population Studies: Reasons for the Late Start

Richard L. Clinton and R. Kenneth Godwin

The reader who has persevered to this point may have far more questions in mind about the interrelations between population and politics than was the case when he began this volume. If this is so, then in an important sense the book has been a success. Some disappointment is justified, however, no matter how many areas for future research have been opened up, for in spite of the stature of the contributors, the lack of depth and experience in the field of population on the part of all but Professors Finkle and Organski—and, of course, Saunders—was often apparent. Hopefully, both their insights and their "blindspots" have demonstrated the potential usefulness of a political scientist's approach to the study of population, yet that this usefulness is still potential evidences the present stage of the discipline's relation to population studies.

Certainly high on the list of questions remaining in the reader's mind should be that of why political scientists have for so long neglected to consider demographic factors either as dependent or independent variables in their analyses of political phenomena. An effort will be made in this chapter to account for this neglect.

To gain a proper perspective on this question it should be recalled at the outset that most other social scientists and, indeed, most governments have been slow to recognize the significance of one of the most important of demographic factors: unchecked population expansion. Joseph Spengler, a recent president of the American Economic Association, was among the first to realize that, in an unexpected sense, the warnings of his discipline's predecessor, Thomas Malthus, were acquiring a fearsome timeliness as the twentieth century unfolded.[1]

The repercussions of population growth rates on capital formation and investment were, of course, obvious to economists long before population increase was seen as a problem.[2] As economic development gradually became a universal goal, however, the implications of a rapid rate of population expansion became increasingly clear, since respectable economic growth rates of 3 to 5 percent per annum were often wiped out or reduced to a marginal 1 or 2 percent annually when calculated on a per capita basis.

In the United States, where the rate of population increase has not been exceptionally high and the immensity of the country and of its endowment of natural resources have until recently disguised the adverse effects of population growth, the seriousness of the problem is only now beginning to be perceived in such peripheral areas as water and air pollution, congestion of the cities and the highways, and the gradual disappearance of certain species of wildlife and of unspoiled areas of natural beauty. It is, of course, a mistake to attribute these ills solely to the increase in population,[3] when in most cases they can be traced to the general inadequacies of our social and political systems, but expanding population is unquestionably a potent factor in exacerbating such problems, and its control would certainly facilitate their solution. This is even more the case as regards the myriad problems of the underdeveloped areas, many of which are not overpopulated in terms of population density, but where the rate of population increase is of such a magnitude that the most strenuous developmental exertions serve only to maintain present levels of poverty.

Belatedly some governments are coming to the realization that the rate of growth of their population is of crucial concern to them[4] and that, to some degree at least, it is susceptible of control. India, Pakistan, and, more recently, South Korea and Taiwan, for example, have made notable efforts to depress their rates of population increase.[5] Such efforts, however, have gone forward largely uninformed by knowledge which might have been provided by social and political research. In the absence of such research, moreover, it has been impossible to determine the extent to which subsequent population changes have in fact resulted from action programs rather than from other factors.

The options open to a government interested in influencing the rate of population growth among its citizens theoretically range from legalization of abortion, dissemination of birth control information and contraceptive devices, active support of family planning clinics, cash incentives for voluntary sterilizations or vasectomies, and concerted programs of antinatalist propaganda to more extreme measures such as raising the age at which marriage may be contracted, instituting fiscal penalties for additional children, and even effecting involuntary mass contraception (e.g., by treating the water supply) and forced sterilization and abortion.[6] Such theoretical means are limited, of course, by technological constraints but also and most importantly by political factors: whether the particular government is autocratic or democratic, totalitarian or pluralistic, energetic or reactive; whether it is sufficiently efficient, adequately financed, and strong enough to make its decisions binding on all its citizens and to override any opposition that might be forthcoming. Obviously the severity of the means employed will also be a function of the perceived seriousness of the threat embodied in the country's rate of population growth. Such perceptions, in turn, depend to a large degree on the political system's capacities for gathering, processing, and interpreting information as well as upon the contextual setting into which action programs will be introduced. To initiate such programs in the absence of research on these matters is certainly to put the cart before the horse.

As slow as most governments, including our own, have been to face up to the implications of an excessive birth rate, the response of political scientists to the political ramifications of population increase has been even slower.[7] Economists and sociologists have, therefore, by default, concerned themselves with the political as well as with the developmental and demographic aspects of population change.[8] While some political scientists have perspicaciously noted that the population explosion constitutes the most formidable problem of their geographical area of concern,[9] and one as early as 1967 devoted an article to the subject,[10] none to date[11] has made the study of the intersection of population and politics his primary research interest.[12] Worse, as the Driver Report cited by Lyle Saunders revealed, as late as 1970 no courses dealing directly with population were offered in any of the twenty political science departments polled.[13] This apparently discipline-wide neglect of population factors in political analyses is the enigma which this chapter seeks to resolve.

Certainly no one would contend that population variables are irrelevant to political phenomena. As demonstrated by Lipsitz' brief survey of political philosophy and, indeed, by Dahl's presidential address to the American Political Science Association in 1967,[14] population size has been considered of political significance by most of the major political thinkers of the past. Could it be that a Bachrachian nondecision[15] has limited the scope of modern political science inquiry so that population matters have been excluded from consideration? Shorn of its cabalistic overtones, the concept of mobilization of bias[16]—broadly construed to include the value structure of the discipline's subculture—might carry us a fair way toward an understanding of this anomaly.

Admittedly the mobilization of bias can be an elusive concept, for it is sometimes difficult to determine precisely where it emerges from a generalized lack of awareness of a given situation. Obviously, political scientists cannot very well be faulted for not having recognized the implications of population changes for their areas of concern when practically everyone else was also oblivious of the far-reaching importance of demographic phenomena. In modern Western society, for instance, population growth has only very recently reached the threshold of awareness of a sizeable sector, hence it could hardly be expected that political scientists would be focusing on a matter which was not yet perceived as a problem—certainly not as in any way a political problem. Although it might seem that scholars specializing in the politics of areas which have serious population problems would have long since recognized the importance of looking at demographic variables, such has not been the case.[17] Asian politics specialists, for example, seem, like the Asians themselves, to have accepted as natural, inevitable, and immutable the high population densities and the problems that result therefrom which have characterized that area of the world for so long. Similarly, political scientists who specialize in the study of Africa or Latin America seem to have assimilated the "psychology of underpopulation" fostered in those regions by the immense areas of uninhabited or very sparsely populated lands.[18]

Such generalized unawareness of the existence of a problem area is not, of course, what is meant by a mobilization of bias. On the contrary the concept comes into play only when, in spite of a pervasive although perhaps not an explicit awareness of a problem area, the problem is still not entered on the agenda of those who should be interested in solving it.

It would certainly seem that one important factor in keeping population variables off the agenda of political scientists has been the strict compartmentalization of knowledge which characterizes the modern university. In this fragmented milieu, moreover, the increasingly narrow specialization within disciplines further exacerbates the problem, for communication among different branches of the same discipline has in many cases become as difficult as (and often more difficult than!) communication between academic fields. This lack of interdisciplinary cross-fertilization seems to have been of considerable significance in the unresponsiveness of political scientists in recognizing the relevance of population variables, for the questions posed by population change are exceptionally interdisciplinary in nature. Particularly as regards population policy, it is all but impossible to separate the psychological, sociological, and philosophical, to say nothing of the economic ramifications of any measure contemplated. Population policies, like all policies, are coercive; but, unlike most other public policies, population policies tend to be seen as intruding into the most intimate and inviolable area of the individual's life. Thus, while the problems of perception, psychological acceptance, and personality consequences of almost any policy are important, psychological variables loom especially large in the process of developing and implementing population policies. Yet such psychological considerations cannot be fruitfully considered in the absence of sociological variables. Any policy which aims at limiting the number of children born, for instance, will inevitably affect the future distributions of ethnic, class, religious, and age groups in society and consequently the relative power and other kinds of relationships among these groups. Moreover, only through sociological analysis of belief systems, mores, and behavior patterns can the strength of many psychological reactions to population policy measures be understood or anticipated. Similarly, philosophical questions cannot be divorced from the issues created by population policies, for seldom is the central dilemma of politics so clearly encountered as in trying to reconcile the *right of the individual* to determine how many children he will have with *the need of the community* to regulate its population size and rate of growth. The whole area concerning the justice of how population policies are conceived and applied, while perhaps no more philosophical than determining the equity of any policy, certainly seems more profoundly philosophical since it deals so directly with human life. Ethical considerations are therefore paramount in both the formulation and implementation and in the analysis and evaluation of population policies.[19]

In addition to its contribution to the interdisciplinary obstacle to the study of the political implications of population by political scientists, the importance of the philosophical-ethical dimension of population policies has presented yet another impediment. Since World War II political science has purposely estranged itself from its parent discipline, political philosophy. The "behavioral revolution" of the postwar period led to excesses which carried the discipline dangerously close to a sterile neo-Scholasticism. The zeal for quantification and for an appearance of scientific rigor resulted in a lengthy period during which methods and data amenable to their use dictated major areas for research. Given this disciplinary mobilization of bias, the likelihood of real-world problems with important philosophical dimensions (such as the politics of population) finding their way onto the lists of needed research by political scientists was drastically reduced. Even now, after some perspective has been regained within significant segments of the discipline, and after the spectrum of both legitimate research topics and methods has been vastly expanded, the discipline-specific problems facing political scientists who wish to specialize in the politics of population are formidable. This is particularly true of the younger political scientist who places himself in a precarious position vis-à-vis the job market by attempting to develop expertise in an area which is not yet a recognized subfield of the discipline. Much the same is true of employed but still untenured political scientists whose promotion depends so disproportionately on their record of publications. One's publication record, of course, consists not merely of the number of articles published but also of the types of publications in which they appeared. Given the competition for space in the leading journals, it is not unreasonable to suspect that a process akin to the mobilization of bias has made and continues to make it far more difficult for an article dealing with population matters to find its way into the pages of reputable political science journals than articles which deal with traditional subfields of the discipline. For the neophyte assistant professor of political science and his hoary colleagues as well, the problem of introducing a new course to deal with the politics of population may also present difficulties, although certainly these will vary greatly from one university to another. The serious aspect of the disciplinary parochialism we have been describing is that the reward structure of the profession is markedly skewed, and the resulting effect is a mobilization of bias which inhibits political science research in population studies.

This "skewness" is apparent in another realm with major implications for the type of research being carried out by political scientists—namely, funding. Until quite recently funding from organizations involved in promoting population-related research was not directed toward political science. Even now most such organizations tend to place severe restrictions on the type of research proposals they would be willing to entertain from political scientists, the most common one being the requirement of a narrow fertility focus. Thus political scientists may be encouraged to study short-term policy effectiveness, but such an approach automatically excludes the majority of practicing political scientists, many of whose interests may be highly relevant to population but in other ways. Too often a political scientist seeking to explore a little understood area of the intersection of population and politics will have his proposal rejected simply because it does not fit any existing category of either political science or population research.

Hopefully we have covered most of the major reasons for political scientists' late entry into population studies. While there is unfortunately no prospect for an immediate improvement in the rigidities of disciplinary boundaries, there does seem to be a somewhat greater realization of the need for multidisciplinary approaches. Certainly there is encouragement to be found in the recent increases in government funds for population research, although much remains to be done in convincing funding agencies of the counterproductiveness of their overly narrow emphasis on fertility and their insistence on immediate "pay-offs." While a host of population-politics questions can be approached quantitatively and thus should appeal to political scientists skilled in computer analysis,[20] there may even be cause for cautious optimism as regards the discipline's self-imposed mobilization of bias against research areas which require explicitly normative approaches. If, in fact, the eternal questions of political philosophy are again becoming fashionable, then political science, in spite of its late start, may yet have more to say about the role of the state in population matters than do "physiology, physics, or plumbing."[21]

Notes

1. See, for instance, his "Aspects of the Economics of Population Growth—Part II," *Southern Economic Journal* 14, no. 3 (January 1948): 233-65, and his presidential address to the American Economic Association, "The Economist and the Population Question," *American Economic Review* 56, no. 1 (March 1966): 1-24.

2. Alvin Hansen, *Economic Stabilization in an Unbalanced World* (New York: Harcourt, Brace and Co., 1932), pp. 229-34. Also see his presidential address to the American Economic Association in 1938, "Economic Progress and Declining Population Growth," *American Economic Review* 29, no. 1, 1 (March 1939): 1-15.

3. This was the theme of an address by Frederick S. Jaffe at a symposium on "Man's Relationship to the Environment as Influenced by Overpopulation," at the University of New Hampshire on September 25, 1969. See also Barry Commoner, *Nature, Man, and Technology* (New York: Alfred A. Knopf, 1971): and Ben Wattenberg, "Overpopulation as a Crisis Issue, The Nonsense Explosion," *The New Republic* (April 4 and 11, 1970), pp. 18-23, reprinted in Daniel Callahan (ed.), *The American Population Debate* (Garden City, N.Y.: Doubleday and Co., Inc., 1971), pp. 96-109.

4. James Reston, "Washington: Who Said 'Love Makes the World Go Round?' " *The New York Times*, 21 January, 1970, p. 40, notes that President Nixon was the first American president to send a message to the Congress

dealing solely with population control. (The message was delivered on July 18, 1969.)

5. The progress of these and other family planning programs is reliably chronicled in the series *Studies in Family Planning, Reports on Population/Family Planning*, and *Current Publications in Population/Family Planning*, all publications of the Population Council, 245 Park Avenue, New York, N.Y. See also the special issue on "Progress and Problems of Fertility Control around the World," *Demography* 5, no. 2 (1968). More up-to-date information on the Chinese situation may be found in Tillman Durdin, "China's Changing Society seems to Cut Birth Rate," *The New York Times*, 21 April, 1971, pp. 1 and 8, and Edgar Snow, "China: Population Care and Control," *The New Republic* (May 1, 1971), pp. 20-23.

6. Bernard Berelson, President of The Population Council, gives an exhaustive review of all the approaches thus far suggested in an article entitled "Beyond Family Planning," *Studies in Family Planning*, no. 38 (February 1969).

7. A.E. Kier Nash, "Pollution, Population, and the Cowboy Economy," *Journal of Comparative Administration* 2, no. 1 (May 1970): 119-20, points out that neither of "the most important new problems of politics in the remainder of this century—pollution and population growth . . . has yet received the attention of a single article in the major national and regional professional [political science] journals."

8. See, for instance, Gunnar Myrdal, *Population: A Problem for Democracy, The Godkin Lectures, 1938* (Cambridge, Mass.: Harvard University Press, 1940); Philip M. Hauser (ed.), *Population and World Politics* (Glencoe, Ill.: The Free Press, 1958); William Petersen, *The Politics of Population* (Garden City, N.Y.: Doubleday and Co., Inc., 1964); Stanislav Andreski, *Parasitism and Subversion: The Case of Latin America* (New York: Schocken Books, 1966), pp. 16-22; Neil W. Chamberlain, *Beyond Malthus: Population and Power* (New York: Basic Books, Inc., 1970); and David Chaplin (ed.) *Population Policies and Growth in Latin America* (Lexington, Mass.: Heath Lexington Books, 1971).

9. Federico G. Gil, *Latin American–United States Relations* (New York: Harcourt Brace Jovanovich, Inc., 1971), p. 245.

10. Russell H. Fitzgibbon, "Political Implications of Population Growth in Latin America," pp. 23-45 of Paul Halmos (ed.) *Latin American Sociological Studies* (Keele University, England: The Sociological Review Monograph no. 11, February, 1967).

11. Of course, the effects of population on international relations have frequently been noted. One book, coauthored by a political scientist and a demographer, although principally concerned with this recurring theme, does touch on other apsects of "the intersection of population and politics," namely, Katherine Organski and A.F.K. Organski, *Population and World Power* (New York: Alfred A. Knopf, 1961).

12. Two of the contributors to this volume, Jason Finkle and A.F.K. Organ-

ski, come closest to being an exception to this assertion; their seminal population-related work has been primarily in the areas of comparative administration
and international relations, respectively. Another eminent representative of the
profession, Myron Weiner of the Massachusetts Institute of Technology, is presently directing his attention to population-related aspects of political inquiry.
Cf. Myron Weiner, "Perceptions of Population Change in India," mimeo, September, 1969, and "Political Demography: An Inquiry into the Political Consequences of Population Change," pp. 567-617 of National Academy of Sciences,
Rapid Population Growth: Consequences and Implications (Baltimore and London: The Johns Hopkins Press, 1971). Since the present study began in mid-
1969, moreover, a number of developments have occurred which seem to point
toward an awakening of political scientists to the challenges of population matters, e.g., the appearance of Nash's indictment of the discipline in May 1970;
The Population Council's Conference on Political Science and Population in
October 1970; the Carolina Population Center's Population-Politics Workshop in
December 1970; and the formation of the International Population Policy Con-
sortium in January 1971. Most encouraging of all is the rapidly increasing number of younger political scientists who are attempting to make a major commitment to population-related teaching and research.

13. So far as we have been able to determine, the first two courses on
population and politics in political science departments were initiated in the fall
of 1971 at the University of North Carolina at Chapel Hill and at Fordham
University.

14. Robert A. Dahl, "The City in the Future of Democracy," *American
Political Science Review* 61, no. 4 (December 1967): 953-70.

15. The provocative concept of the "non-decision" is developed in two articles by Peter Bachrach and Morton S. Baratz, "Two Faces of Power," *American
Political Science Review* 56, no. 4 (December 1962): 947-52, and "Decisions
and Nondecisions: An Analytic Framework," *American Political Science Review*
57, no. 3 (September 1963): 632-42.

16. See chapter 4, "The Displacement of Conflicts," in E.E. Schattschneider,
The Semisovereign People: A Realist's View of Democracy in America (New
York: Holt, Rinehart and Winston, 1960).

17. To their credit, however, area specialists do appear to be disproportionately represented in the vanguard of political scientists engaged in population
research.

18. See Richard Lee Clinton, *Problems of Population Policy Formation in
Peru* (Chapel Hill: The Carolina Population Center, Population Program and
Policy Design Series: no. 4, 1971), pp. 146-48.

19. This issue is insightfully treated in a larger context by Beryl L. Crowe,
"The Tragedy of the Commons Revisited," *Science* 166, no. 3909 (28 November
1969): 1103-107.

20. An outstanding example of the usefulness of demographic data and tech-

niques in political research is the recent book by Butler and Stokes which employs cohort analysis and differential fertility and mortality rates to explain variations in the support for and success of British political parties. David Butler and Donald Stokes, *Political Change in Britain: Forces Shaping Electoral Choice* (New York: St. Martin's Press, 1969). See especially pp. 50, 56, 62-64, and 263-74.

21. See p. 42 of Theodore Lowi's chapter in this book.

Index

151

About the Contributors

Peter Bachrach, professor of political science at Temple University in Philadelphia, received his Ph.D. from Harvard in 1951. His major research interests are political theory and public policy. Among his many scholarly publications two of the most recent are *The Theory of Democratic Elitism: A Critique* (Little, Brown, 1967), and, with Morton B. Baratz, *Power and Poverty: Theory and Practice* (Oxford University Press, 1970).

Bruce Bueno de Mesquita, assistant professor of political science at Michigan State University, received his Ph.D. from the University of Michigan in 1971. His major research interests are in the areas of quantitative international politics, conflict resolution, and political development.

Richard L. Clinton is assistant professor of political science at the University of North Carolina, Chapel Hill, where he earned his Ph.D. in 1971. His fields of special interest are Latin American politics, political theory, and the as yet undefined area of the political implications of population change. His publications have appeared in *The Journal of Inter-American Studies and World Affairs, Inter-American Economic Affairs,* and *The Annals of the Southeastern Conference on Latin American Studies.*

Jason Finkle is professor in the Department of Population Planning of the University of Michigan, where he took his Ph.D. in 1959. His primary research and teaching concerns are with the interrelationships between population and development. In addition to having contributed to a number of collected works and the *Journal of Comparative Administration*, Professor Finkle is coeditor, with Richard W. Gable, of the widely used volume *Political Development and Social Change* (Wiley, 1966; 2nd ed., 1971) and is editor of a forthcoming book entitled *The Population Controversy and Public Policy.*

William S. Flash is associate professor of health administration and lecturer in political science at the University of North Carolina, Chapel Hill. He earned his Ph.D. in political science at Harvard in 1954 and has specialized in public administration of health and population policies. His publications have appeared in such journals as *Public Administration Review* and *Servicios Públicos.*

Moye W. Freymann is director of the Carolina Population Center at the University of North Carolina, Chapel Hill. He received his M.D. from Johns Hopkins University in 1948 and, after public health experience in Iran and India, completed his Dr.P.H. at Harvard in 1960. He has contributed chapters to a large number of books and reports.

R. Kenneth Godwin, assistant professor of political science at Oregon State University, received his Ph.D. from the University of North Carolina, Chapel Hill in 1971. His major research interests are political behavior and comparative politics, particularly the problems of measurement encountered in devising survey instruments and interpreting survey data. Professor Godwin is a contributor to and co-editor, with Richard Clinton, of a forthcoming volume entitled *Research in the Politics of Population* (Heath-Lexington Books, 1972).

Allan Lamborn is a doctoral student in political science at the University of Michigan. His major area of concentration is international politics.

Alden Lind is currently a postdoctoral fellow at Yale University. He received his Ph.D. in political science in 1966 from the University of Oregon. In addition to his interests in state and local government and in computer applications to political research, Dr. Lind has built a special competence in the area of political psychology.

Lewis Lipsitz, associate professor of political science at the University of North Carolina, Chapel Hill, earned his Ph.D. at Yale University in 1964. His teaching and research interests are in the fields of political philosophy and empirical political theory. Professor Lipsitz's publications have appeared in the *American Political Science Review*, the *American Sociological Review, Polity*, and in a number of collected works.

Theodore J. Lowi, professor of political science at the University of Chicago, received his Ph.D. in 1961 from Yale. His principal research interests are in the area of public policy. He is a frequent contributor to the *American Political Science Review*. His most recent books include *The End of Liberalism* (Norton, 1969), and *Arenas of Power—A Reconstruction of American Politics* (forthcoming).

A.F.K. Organski is professor of political science and program director of the Institute for Social Research at the University of Michigan. He received his Ph.D. from New York University in 1951. Professor Organski is primarily concerned with the theoretical aspects of international politics and the relation of population to world politics. His best known books are *World Politics* (Knopf, 1958; 2nd ed. 1968), *Population and World Power* (with Katherine Organski; Knopf, 1961), and *Stages of Political Development* (Knopf, 1965).

Lyle Saunders, a medical sociologist, is a program advisor in population and family planning at the Ford Foundation's office in Bangkok, Thailand, having served in this capacity in various areas of Africa, Asia, and Latin America. He is the author of several books and articles dealing with the medical and social aspects of fertility control.

DATE DUE
